Sew a Circle
of Friends

Sew a Circle of Friends

Adorable Cloth Doll Projects

Anne McKinney

Sterling Publishing Co., Inc. New York
A Sterling/Chapelle Book

Chapelle, Ltd.

Owner: Jo Packham

Editor: Laura Best

Staff: Marie Barber, Malissa Boatwright, Kass Burchett, Rebecca Christensen, Holly Fuller, Marilyn Goff, Michael Hannah, Shirley Heslop, Holly Hollingsworth, Susan Jorgensen, Susan Laws, Pauline Locke, Ginger Mikkelsen, Barbara Milburn, Linda Orton, Karmen Quinney, Leslie Ridenour, Cindy Rooks, and Cindy Stoeckl

Photographer: Kevin Dilley for Hazen Photography

Photography Styling: Susan Laws

Dedication

This book is dedicated to my daughters, Hannah and Claire, who bless and inspire me every single day!

Special thanks to Jeff Ray of Tuesday Publishing

Library of Congress Cataloging-in-Publication Data Available

A Sterling/Chapelle Book

10 9 8 7 6 5 4 3 2 1

First paperback edition published in 1998 by
Sterling Publishing Company, Inc.
387 Park Avenue South, New York, N.Y. 10016
© 1997 by Chapelle, Ltd.
Distributed in Canada by Sterling Publishing
c/o Canadian Manda Group, One Atlantic Avenue, Suite 105
Toronto, Ontario, Canada M6K 3E7
Distributed in Great Britain and Europe by Cassell PLC
Wellington House, 125 Strand, London WC2R 0BB, England
Distributed in Australia by Capricorn Link (Australia) Pty Ltd.
P.O. Box 6651, Baulkham Hills, Business Centre, NSW 2153,
Australia
Printed in Hong Kong
All rights reserved

Sterling ISBN 0-8069-8611-5 Trade
           0-8069-8702-2 Paper

If you have any questions or comments or would like information on specialty products featured in this book, please contact:

Chapelle, Ltd.
P.O. Box 9252
Ogden, UT 84409
(801) 621-2777
(801) 621-2788 Fax

About the Author...

Anne McKinney is a doll designer, company owner, and stay at home mom. Tucked away in rural Ohio, Anne stays busy with her wholesale folk art doll and accessory company, *My Sister's Closet*, which has been in business since 1986. Anne also works in the public market through her company *Circle of Friends*. Anne went public with *Circle of Friends* in 1994 due to high demand and public recognition through her products sold in the *Gooseberry Patch* mail order catalog. Through *Circle of Friends*, just as in this book, Anne has made patterns and projects available for the home crafter.

Though busy with her companies, Anne's first love is her family: husband Michael and daughters, Hannah and Claire. Her determination to "be there for her girls" has been the driving force in keeping her continually growing businesses at home.

Anne relies on Deb Strain, who has become an integral part of the pattern company. Deb has a special talent for capturing the whimsical features of each doll and product. Deb has ventured out to form *Saltbox Illustrations* which consists of wonderful paper products including many of the *Circle of Friends* characters.

A complete catalog of *Circle of Friends* products can be obtained by writing to Circle of Friends, 4896 Delisle Fourman Rd., Greenville, Ohio 45331.

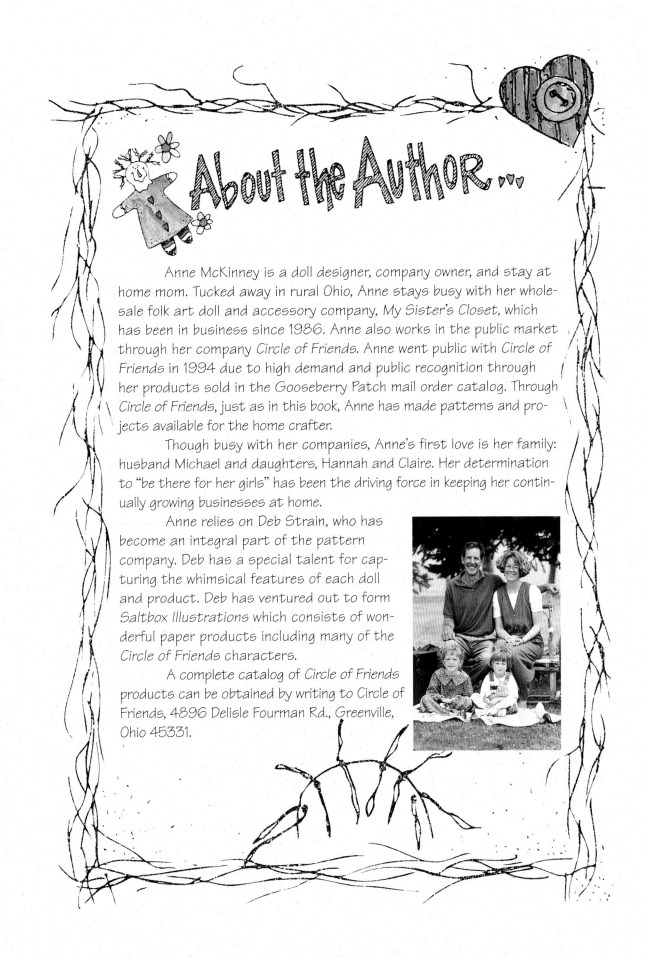

CONTENTS

GENERAL INSTRUCTIONS

Embroidery Stitches

French Knot
(1) Bring needle up through fabric at A. Smoothly wrap floss twice around needle (unless otherwise noted).
(2) Hold floss securely off to one side and push needle down through fabric at B. Pull needle to back.
(3) Completed French Knot.

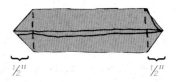

Lazy Daisy Stitch
(1) Bring needle up at A. Keep floss flat, untwisted, and full. Poke needle down through fabric at B and up at C, keeping thread under needle tip forming a loop. Pull thread through, leaving loop loose and full. To hold loop in place, go down on other side of thread near C, forming a straight stitch over loop.
(2) Completed Lazy Daisy Stitch.

Primitive Running Stitch
A line of straight stitches with an unstitched area between each stitch. Come up at (A) and down at (B).

Satin Stitch
(1) Come up at A and go down at B. Come back up at C next to A and go down at D. Keep floss flat and fill in solid.
(2) Completed Satin Stitch.

Straight Stitch
(1) Come up at A and go down at B.
(2) Completed Straight Stitch.

Patterns

Paper Bag Bottom
After sewing body piece right sides together, bring side seams and bottom seam together and measure ½" from corners. Sew across lines forming a rectangle on bottom (see Paper Bag Diagram).

Paper Bag Diagram

½"   ½"

Crow
Roll a piece of oven-bake clay into a 1" snake about ½" in diameter. Flatten one end of roll on hard surface to form tail. Roll other end into a blunt point for beak. Bake according to manufacturer's instructions. Paint entire piece black and let dry. Paint gold beak at pointed end. Make a white dot for eye on each side of head. When dry, make a black dot in center of eye.

Clay Sunflower
Make 8 tiny balls of oven-bake clay for petals and one larger ball for center of flower. Flatten larger ball and mash smaller ball around to form flower. Bake according to manufacturer's instructions. When cool, paint gold with a brown center. Paint assorted black dots in center.

Robin
Roll a small ball of oven-bake clay (⅜" diameter). Lay ball on table and pinch side to form wings and tail. Make a small pinch on other side to make beak. Bake according to manufacturer's instructions. Let cool. Paint bottom red, beak gold, and rest of body brown. Dot on eyes with black pigment pen.

Hints

Blush Cheeks
Select favorite powdered blush and carefully apply to cheeks with tip of a cotton swab. An old worn paintbrush can be used in place of cotton swab.

Carpet Thread
Recommended for sewing openings closed and gathering material. Dental floss also works well.

Display
To hang doll for displaying, secure a loop of carpet thread at back of neck.

Enlarging
Using a photocopy machine, enlarge pattern pieces to percentage listed on each piece.

Faces
Instructions call for faces to be drawn after doll is stuffed. Faces may be applied before stuffing, if the face does not turn out as hoped additional work need not be put into the project.

Floss
Separate floss strands then use two at a time unless otherwise stated in instructions.

Fusible Applique
Trace pattern shapes onto paper side of fusible webbing. Cut out around shapes leaving about ¼" outside line. Iron onto wrong side of fabric, using a warm dry iron for 2-3 seconds. After piece cools, cut out exactly on line. Peel off backing paper. Position onto background, fusible web side down. Iron into place following manufacturer's instructions.

Imagination
These projects are a reflection of the maker and the recipient. Choose accessories, materials, and colors to reflect the meaning. There is no wrong way to embellish. Let the giver's or the recipient's personality show through!

Kitty Litter
Pour into bottom of doll to help stand. Bird seed or fine gravel can be replaced for kitty litter.

Personalize
Sign and date a doll on bottom of foot or hem of apron. A small verse or friend's name along wings or skirt hem makes a doll extra special.

Pigment Pen
Marking pen, found at most craft stores, containing pigment. Permanent marking pen can also be used, but color is not as brilliant.

Stuffing
When using polyester stuffing, always use little pieces of stuffing and methodically stuff from tip to opening. If pieces are too large, project will appear lumpy.

Tea-dying
Bring 2-3 cups of water to a boil. Turn off heat and put in 8 tea bags. Let steep for 30 minutes. Place fabric in tea water and soak for 30-45 minutes. Rinse slightly, wring out, and let dry, or throw in dryer. Make certain to wipe out dryer with a wet rag after use.

Transfer Tools
Used to transfer pattern onto material. Necessary supplies would include something to transfer with (dress maker's pen, fabric pen, transfer pencil or disappearing pen) and something to make a template from (mylar or heavy cardboard).

Transferring
One method of transferring is to trace pattern onto tracing paper. Cut out and use as pattern to trace onto mylar for template. Transfer all markings, such as openings and button placement. Another way to transfer is to tape lightweight paper to window over pattern and trace using sunlight. Cut out pattern and then trace onto mylar or cardboard. Use mylar pattern to cut out material. Cut slightly larger than pattern because no seam allowance has been added in instructions.

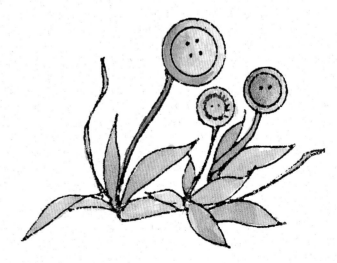

ANGELS IN THE GARDEN

Sunflower

Materials
- Cotton fabric: blue, ⅓ yd. (dress)
- Homespun: 2 or 3 scraps
- Muslin: ⅓ yd. (body)
- Print fabric: 5" x 10" (apron)
- Needle: hand-stitching
- Stuffing
- Thread: carpet; coordinating
- Cinnamon stick: 1
- Greenery: 9" piece (garland)
- Greens
- Miniature garden tools: 2 or 3
- Sinamy hat: 4"
- Sunflower seeds
- Tansy: dried
- Wavy wool hair: blonde, 3½"
- Wood sunflowers: unpainted, 1" (3)
- Paint: black; dk. brown; gold
- Pigment pens: black, .01; red, .01
- Transfer tools
- Oven-bake clay: white
- Hot glue gun and glue sticks
- Iron and ironing board
- Paintbrush: fine-tip
- Scissors
- Sewing machine
- Cotton swabs
- Powdered blush

Read all instructions before beginning.

Body
Trace around body, leg, and arm patterns (see pg. 14) on doubled piece of muslin. Sew on line. Cut out and turn right side out. Stuff arms to within 1" of end. Stuff legs to within 1" of top. Stuff head and body to within 2" of bottom of body. Insert legs into body with toes pointing forward. Stitch across bottom of body and across legs using carpet thread. Make a running stitch across top of arms. Draw up tightly and attach to shoulders.

Dress
Trace around bodice pattern (see pg. 15). Cut bodice out of blue fabric. Sew along seam lines on pattern. Turn under neck and sleeve edges. Run a gathering stitch with carpet thread along neckline and on each sleeve edge. Put top on doll and draw up thread. Knot off and tie in bow. Cut one 6" x 22" piece of blue fabric for skirt. Sew a seam along 6" side with right sides together. Hem bottom on sewing machine. Turn under ¼" and run a gathering stitch along top of skirt. Draw up tightly around waist, over bodice. Tie off tightly.

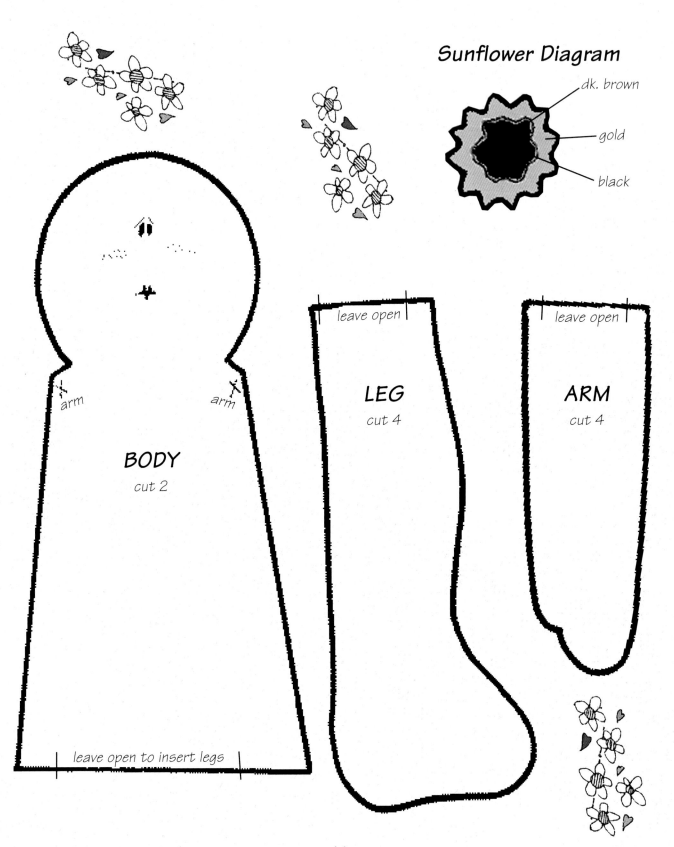

Sunflower Diagram

dk. brown

gold

black

BODY
cut 2

arm

arm

leave open to insert legs

LEG
cut 4

leave open

ARM
cut 4

leave open

14

Apron

Turn top edge of 5" x 10" printed fabric under ¾" and machine or hand-stitch a gathering stitch ½" from top edge with carpet thread. Gather fabric and tie around waist.

Face & Hair

Draw face with black and red pigment pens following features on body pattern. Color cheeks with blush and a cotton swab. Sew blonde wool hair on top of head. Pull apart braid to fluff out. Turn back front of hat and secure with glue. Glue on tansy, greens, and sunflower seeds. Glue hat over hair.

Finishing Touches

Paint wood sunflowers using Sunflower Diagram. Let dry. Space sunflowers evenly across the 9" garland, centering one sunflower. Fill in garland with pieces of cinnamon stick, small pieces of knotted homespun, and miniature garden tools. Glue one end to each hand. Make a clay sunflower (see General Instructions pg. 8). Glue clay sunflower to neck.

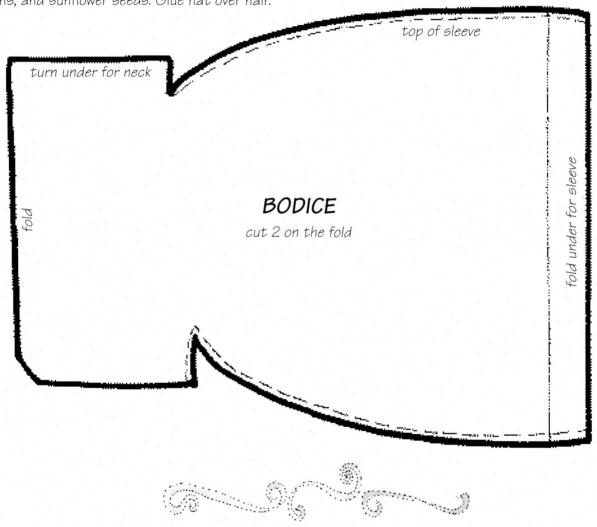

top of sleeve

turn under for neck

fold

fold under for sleeve

BODICE
cut 2 on the fold

Never burden friends with secrets.
— Rabbi Matthew Finegood

Materials

Flannel: cotton, ⅓ yd.
Homespun: ⅛ yd. (heart & band)
Muslin: tea-dyed, ⅓ yd. (body)
Ribbon: chiffon, wired, 1" wide, ½ yd.
Buttons: assorted, tiny (4)
Floss: green; pink; yellow
Needles: embroidery; hand-stitching
Stuffing
Thread: carpet; coordinating; linen
Artificial flower: dried (hair)
Artificial leaves: small, green
Charm: brass locket key
Doilies: white, round, 4"; lace, round, 8"
Wavy wool hair: blonde, 3"
Disappearing transfer pen
Pigment pens: black, .01; red, .01
Transfer tools
Hot glue gun and glue sticks
Iron and ironing board
Scissors
Sewing machine
Cotton swabs
Powdered blush

Read all instructions before beginning.

Body

Trace around body, leg, and arm patterns (see pg. 18) on doubled piece of muslin. Sew on line. Cut out and turn right side out. Stuff arms to within 1" of end. Stuff legs to within 1" of top. Stuff head and body to within 2" of bottom of body. Insert legs into body with toes pointing forward. Stitch across bottom of body and across legs using carpet thread. Make a running stitch across top of arms. Draw up tightly and attach to shoulders.

Dress

Trace around bodice pattern (see pg. 19). Cut bodice out of flannel. Sew along seam lines on pattern. Turn under neck and sleeve edges. Run a gathering stitch with carpet thread along neckline and on each sleeve edge. Put top on doll and draw up thread. Knot off and tie in bow. Cut one 4" x 22" piece of flannel for skirt. Cut one 4" x 22" piece of homespun for band. Fold band in half with wrong sides together. Stitch to flannel skirt. Press seam up and top-stitch onto flannel. Sew a seam along 4" side of skirt with right sides together. Hem bottom on sewing machine.

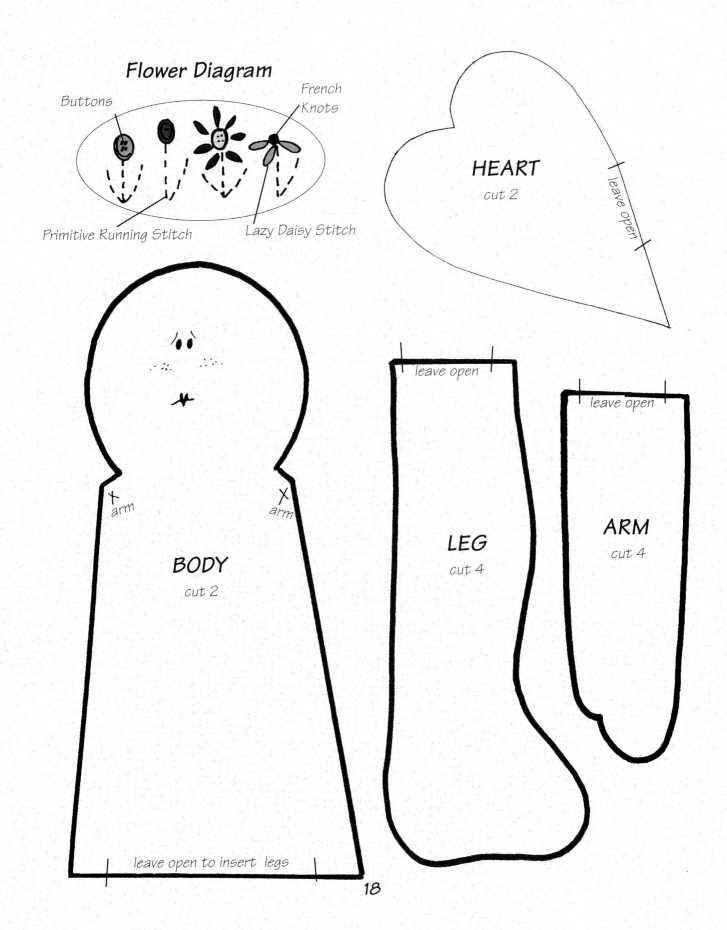

Flower Diagram

Buttons

French Knots

Primitive Running Stitch

Lazy Daisy Stitch

HEART
cut 2

leave open

arm

arm

BODY
cut 2

leave open to insert legs

LEG
cut 4

leave open

ARM
cut 4

leave open

18

Skirt Flowers

Using a disappearing transfer pen, copy Flower Diagram onto bottom of skirt. Using floss and tiny buttons, embroider flowers following pattern instructions. Turn under top edge ¼" and run a gathering stitch along top of skirt. Draw up tightly around waist, over bodice. Tie off tightly.

Collar

Cut a 2½" slit in center of 4" crocheted doily. Pull over head, tucking under stray ends. Tie brass locket key around neck with carpet thread and tie off in a bow.

Face & Hair

Draw face with black and red pigment pens following features on body pattern. Color cheeks with blush and a cotton swab. Sew blonde wool hair on top of head. Pull apart braid to fluff out. Glue on a few green leaves and a dried flower.

Wings

Fold 8" lace doily in half and make a finger crease down center. Open doily back up and make a running stitch from one side to the other along crease. Draw up as tightly as possible and stitch to secure. Glue onto back of doll beginning at base of neck.

Heart

Trace heart pattern onto a doubled piece of homespun. Sew on line leaving an opening where indicated. Cut out and turn right sides out. Stuff firmly and close opening. Sew a button to front of heart. Tie off in a bow with linen thread. Sew onto hand with carpet thread.

Finishing Touches

Tie a large bow using wired ribbon and glue to waist.

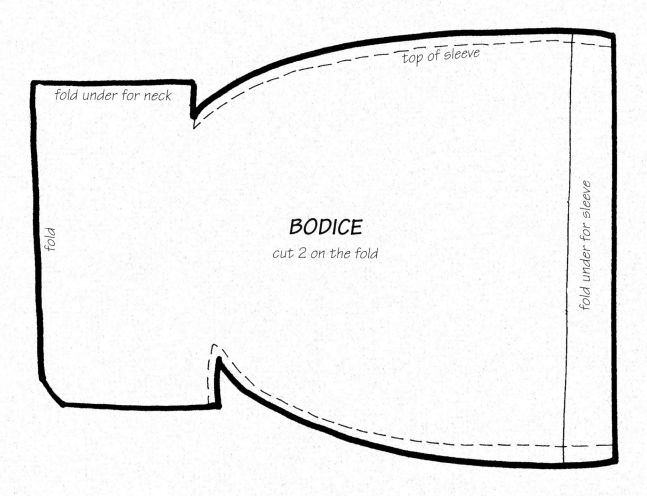

fold under for neck

top of sleeve

fold

fold under for sleeve

BODICE

cut 2 on the fold

Materials

- Cotton fabric: ¼ yd. (dress)
- Muslin: ¼ yd. (body)
- Needle: hand-stitching
- Stuffing
- Thread: carpet; coordinating
- Charm: tin birdhouse or heart
- Curly braid: red, 3"
- Doilies: crocheted, round, 4"; lace, round, 8"
- Greenery: pine, few sprigs
- Resin flower (hair)
- Paint: colors of dress fabric
- Pigment pen: black, .01; red, .01
- Transfer tools
- Balsa wood: ½" x 4"
- Tin: scrap, ¹⁄₁₆" thick
- Wire: small gauge, 24" (garland)
- Nails: small
- Craft knife
- Hammer
- Hot glue gun and glue sticks
- Iron and ironing board
- Paintbrush: fine tip
- Scissors
- Sewing machine
- Wire cutters
- Cotton swabs
- Powdered blush

Read all instructions before beginning.

Body

Trace around body, leg, and arm patterns (see pg. 22) on doubled piece of muslin. Sew on line. Cut out and turn right side out. Stuff arms to within 1" of end. Stuff legs to within 1" of top. Stuff head and body to within 2" of bottom of body. Insert legs into body with toes pointing forward. Stitch across bottom of body and across legs using carpet thread. Make a running stitch across top of arms. Draw up tightly and attach to shoulders.

Dress

Trace around bodice pattern (see pg. 23). Cut bodice out of cotton fabric. Sew along seam lines on pattern. Turn under neck and sleeve edges. Run a gathering stitch with carpet thread along neckline and on each sleeve edge. Put top on doll and draw up thread. Knot off and tie in a bow. Cut one 6" x 22" piece of cotton fabric for skirt. Sew a seam along 6" side with right sides together. Hem bottom on sewing machine. Turn under top edge ¼" and run a gather stitch along top of skirt. Draw up tightly around waist, over bodice. Tie off tightly.

21

Collar

Cut a 2½" slit in center of 4" crocheted doily. Pull over head, tucking under stray ends. Tie tin birdhouse around neck with carpet thread and tie off in a bow.

Face & Hair

Draw face with black and red pigment pens following features on body pattern. Color cheeks with blush and a cotton swab. Sew red curly braid on top of head. Pull apart braid to fluff out. Glue a few sprigs of pine greenery on hair. Glue resin flower in center of forehead.

Wings

Fold 8" lace doily in half and make a finger crease down center. Open doily back up and make a running stitch from one side to the other along crease. Draw up as tightly as possible and stitch to secure. Glue onto back of doll beginning at base of neck.

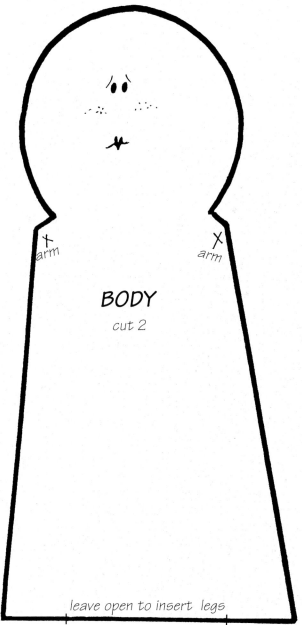

arm

arm

BODY

cut 2

leave open to insert legs

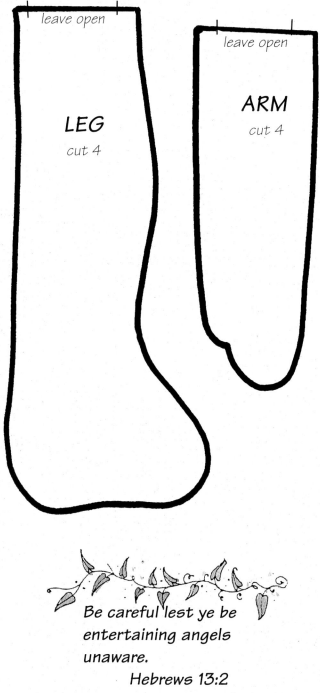

leave open

LEG

cut 4

leave open

ARM

cut 4

Be careful lest ye be
entertaining angels
unaware.

Hebrews 13:2

22

Birdhouses

Make three birdhouses for garland. Start with a piece of balsa wood ½" wide. Cut three 1" pieces (one for each birdhouse). Use varied shapes. The roof pieces are ¾" x ¾" tin squares glued onto the slant of the roofs. Make slants of roofs different to get varied looks. Make holes in fronts by poking wire into wood. Since balsa wood is so soft a craft knife can be used for cutting. In each house, pound in a small nail for perch and clip off head with wire cutters. Paint houses three colors that complement doll's dress. Allow houses to dry. Slide birdhouses onto small gauge wire. If using balsa wood, poke wire through body of birdhouse. If using a harder wood, drill a hole through each house first. Bend wire around a pen or a small diameter item to make curls. After completing garland, make a loop at each end. Securely sew one end to each hand.

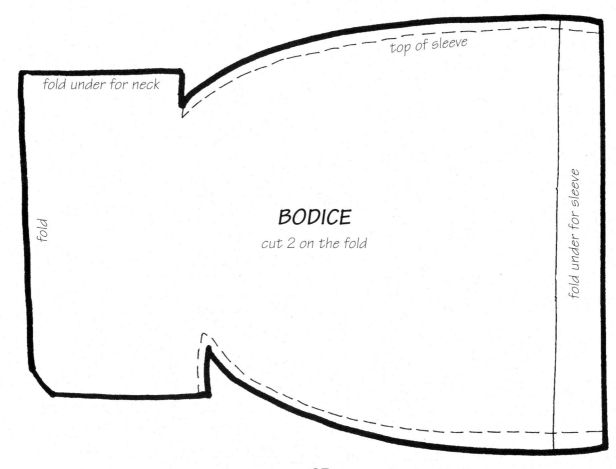

fold under for neck

top of sleeve

fold

fold under for sleeve

BODICE

cut 2 on the fold

23

PHOEBE

Materials

Cotton fabric: ⅓ yd.
Muslin: ½ yd. (body)
Lace: ½", soft, white (18")
Buttons: ½", flat (3); ½", fancy (1)
Needle: hand-stitching
Stuffing
Thread: carpet; coordinating
Boxwood or green leaves: 24
Doily: white, round, 8" (wings)
Greens: various
Rosebuds: 4
Spanish moss
Paint: black; brown; gold; off-white
Disappearing transfer pen
Pigment pen: black, .01
Transfer tools
Wood block: ½"
Tin: scrap
Wire: small gauge
Oven-bake clay: white
Basket: 3"
Hot glue gun and glue sticks
Iron and ironing board
Paintbrush: fine tip
Scissors
Sewing machine
Tin snips
Cotton swabs
Powdered blush

Read all instructions before beginning.

Body

Trace around body, leg, and arm patterns (see pg. 27) on doubled piece of muslin. Sew on line. Cut out and turn right side out. Stuff arms to within 1" of end. Stuff legs to within 1" of top. Stuff head and body to within 2" of bottom of body. Insert legs into body with toes pointing forward. Stitch across bottom of body and across legs using carpet thread. Make a running stitch across top of arms. Draw up tightly and attach to shoulders.

Dress

Trace around bodice pattern (see pg. 26). Cut bodice out of cotton fabric. Sew along seam lines on pattern. Turn under neck and sleeve edges. Run a gathering stitch with carpet thread along neckline and on each sleeve edge. Put top on doll and

25

draw up thread. Knot off and tie in a bow. Cut one 6" x 22" piece of cotton fabric for skirt. Sew a seam along 6" side with right sides together. Hem bottom on sewing machine. Turn under top edge ¼" and run a gathering stitch along top of skirt. Draw up tightly around waist, over bodice. Tie off tightly.

Ears

Trace around ear pattern (see pg. 27). Stitch around traced pattern on line, leave opening where indicated. Cut out and turn ride side out. Press open ends to inside ¼". Press flat and hand-sew ears to head where shown on body pattern.

Face & Hair

Draw face with black pigment pen following features on body pattern. Color cheeks with blush and a cotton swab. Run a doubled piece of carpet thread on each side of nose to make whiskers.

Necklace

Using carpet thread and a needle, string 5 leaves, 1 rosebud, 3 leaves, and 1 button. Continue pattern two more times. Tie around neck and tie off in a bow at back.

Wings

Fold 8" lace doily in half and make a finger crease down center. Open doily back up and make a running stitch from one side to the other along crease. Draw up as tightly as possible and knot off. Stitch to secure. Glue onto back of doll beginning at base of neck.

Birdhouse

Paint ½" wood block off-white and let dry. With pigment pen, make a hole and write 'Welcome' around the hole. Cut strip of tin ⅝" x 1½". Center tin over two sides of block and bend to form roof. Glue tin securely to block.

Basket

Fill basket with Spanish moss and greens. Glue birdhouse in basket. Make 2 clay sunflowers (see General Instructions pg. 8). Glue sunflowers on wires and put into basket. Add 2 rosebuds and fill in with greenery. Sew handle of basket securely to bunny's hand.

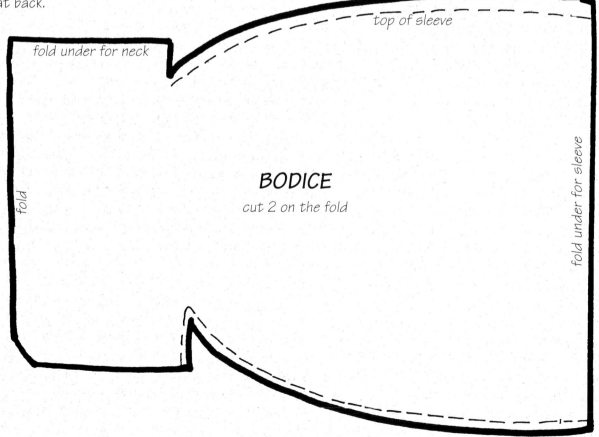

top of sleeve

fold under for neck

fold under for sleeve

fold

BODICE

cut 2 on the fold

Finishing Touches

Tie a small bow out of soft white lace. Glue a few sprigs of greenery and bow together between the ears. Glue a fancy button in center of bow. Tie a bit larger lace bow and glue off to one side of skirt.

ear   ear

BODY

cut 2

arm   arm

leave open to insert legs

leave open

ARM

cut 4

LEG

cut 4

leave open

EAR

cut 4

leave open

Gert

Materials
- Cotton fabric: small scrap (bag)
- Muslin: tea-dyed, 6" x 18" (body)
- Lace: crocheted, ⅜" wide (1 yd.)
- Ribbon: chiffon, wired, scrap (hat)
- Button: antique, small
- Needle: hand-stitching
- Stuffing
- Thread: carpet; coordinating
- Boxwood
- Miniature flower pot with flowers
- Spanish moss
- Sweet Annie
- Tansy
- Wool roving: grey (hair)
- Paint: black; dk. gold; primrose pink; yellow; white
- Pigment pens: black, .01; red, .01
- Transfer tools
- Covered wire
- Oven-bake clay: white
- Straw hat: 2"
- Hot glue gun and glue sticks
- Paintbrush: fine tip
- Scissors
- Sewing machine
- Cotton swabs
- Kitty litter: ½ cup
- Powdered blush

Read all instructions before beginning.

Body
Trace body pattern (see pg. 30) on doubled piece of muslin. Sew on line, leaving opening where indicated. Cut out and make a paper bag bottom (see General Instructions pg. 8). Turn right side out. Fill bottom with kitty litter then stuff firmly. Hand-stitch opening closed.

Dress
Following body pattern (see pg. 30), paint body primrose pink. Let dry. Glue a strip of lace down front of body. Glue a piece around neckline. Glue button on at center of neckline.

Face & Hair
Draw face with black and red pigment pens following features on body pattern. Color cheeks with blush and a cotton swab. Sew grey hair on top of head. Pull apart braid to fluff out.

Bumblebee

Roll a small amount of oven-bake clay into a ball. Flatten top and bottom to form an oval. With thumb and forefinger, push in at sides (see Diagram 1). Bake according to manufacturer's directions. Let cool. Paint yellow and black stripes on back. Paint black oval in front for face. Paint eyes white with black dots in middle.

Hat

Glue a small amount of Spanish moss to brim of straw hat. Glue bumblebee to peek over brim. Tie wired ribbon into a knot and glue to back of hat. Glue hat on head.

Flower

Paint a small piece of muslin (about 6" x 6") off-white, front and back. When dry, trace two of flower pattern onto muslin. Cut out carefully. Lay one flower on top of other, putting petals in between each other. Sew two layers together in a circle shape. Paint center dark gold. Glue a doubled piece of covered wire on back.

Bag

Cut bag pattern out of cotton fabric. Fold in half with right sides together and sew along side and bottom. Turn right side out. Put a small amount of stuffing in bottom. Make a running stitch with carpet thread about ¼" down from top raw edge. Stick in sweet Annie, tansy, boxwood, and flower made above. Draw up string bag and tie a bow. Glue onto body. Glue flower pot with flowers at base of body.

Diagram 1

Flower Pattern
cut 2

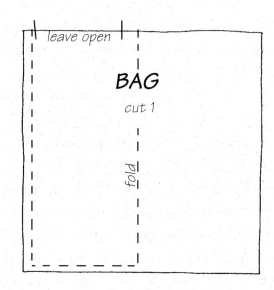

BAG

cut 1

leave open

fold

BODY

cut 2

leave open

Harriett

Materials

Homespun: scrap
Muslin: tea-dyed, ⅛ yd. (body)
Raffia
Button: ½"
Needle: hand-stitching
Stuffing
Thread: coordinating
Greens: variety
Miniatures: gourd; seed packet
Poppy seeds
Spanish moss
Sweet Annie
Yarrow
Paint: black; brown; gold; green;
       burnt orange; red; white
Pigment pen: black, .01
Transfer tools
Wood block: ½"
Oven-bake clay: white
Basket: 1"
Straw hat: 2"
Hot glue gun and glue sticks
Paintbrush: fine tip
Paring knife
Scissors
Sewing machine
Cotton swabs
Kitty litter: ½ cup
Powdered blush

Read all instructions before beginning.

Body

Trace body pattern (see pg. 33) on doubled piece of muslin. Sew on line, leaving an opening where indicated. Cut out and make a paper bag bottom (see General Instructions pg. 8). Turn right side out. Fill bottom with kitty litter. Put small amount of stuffing in each hand; leave arms unstuffed. Sew a running stitch across ears and draw up tightly. Stuff head and body firmly. Hand-stitch opening closed.

Apron

Cut a scrap of homespun 1½" x 3½". Gather along one long edge and draw up. Glue to bunny at waist. Glue button at waist over apron.

Clay Pumpkin

Make 4 clay pumpkins. For each pumpkin, roll a small ball of oven-bake clay (⅜"). With paring knife make slit marks vertically along sides to give pumpkin shape. Roll a tiny bit of clay for stem and press on top center. Bake following manufacturer's instructions. Paint stem brown and pumpkin burnt orange. Let dry. Detail pumpkin lines with black pigment pen.

Face & Hair

Draw face with black pigment pen following features on body pattern. Color cheeks with blush and a cotton swab. Glue ears down to sides of head. Glue on straw hat. Decorate hat with greens, yarrow, 2 pumpkins and a robin (see General Instructions pg. 8).

Basket

Bring paws to front. Slip basket over one paw. Glue paw to top corner of apron. Fill basket with a gourd, a pumpkin, and Spanish moss. Glue raffia bow onto handle. Glue poppy seeds on top of wood block. Paint seeds red for berries. Let dry. Glue 'berry box' to top of paw.

Finishing Touches

Glue free paw to other corner of apron. Fill arm with sweet Annie and other greens. Glue a seed packet and pumpkin on paw. Tie a small strip of homespun in a bow and glue at neck.

One man gives freely, yet gains even more; another withholds unduly, but comes to poverty. A generous man will prosper; he who refreshes others will himself be refreshed.
Proverbs 121: 24, 25

BODY
cut 2

apron line

leave open

33

Myrtle

Materials
Fabric: blue print, 4" x 12"
Muslin: ⅛ yd. (body)
Lace: flat, scrap
Raffia
Button: white
Needle: hand-stitching
Stuffing
Thread: carpet; coordinating
Charm: HERBS sign, small
Cinnamon star
Drieds: small
Miniatures: gardening tools;
     seed packet
Spanish moss
Sunflower seeds
Sweet Annie
Yarrow
Paint: black; blue; brown; gold
Pigment pen: black, .01
Transfer tools
Wire: covered, brown
Oven-bake clay: white
Basket: 1"
Straw hat: 2"
Hot glue gun and glue sticks
Paintbrush: fine tip
Scissors
Sewing machine
Cotton swabs
Kitty litter: ¾ cup
Powdered blush

Read all instructions before beginning.

Body
Enlarge body pattern (see pg. 35). Trace pattern on doubled piece of muslin. Sew on line, leaving an opening where indicated. Cut out and make a paper bag bottom (see General Instructions pg. 8). Turn right side out. Fill bottom with kitty litter. Put a small amount of stuffing in each hand. Leave arms unstuffed. Make a running stitch across ears and draw up tightly. Stuff head and body firmly. Hand-stitch opening closed. Referring to body pattern, paint upper body blue for bodice of dress.

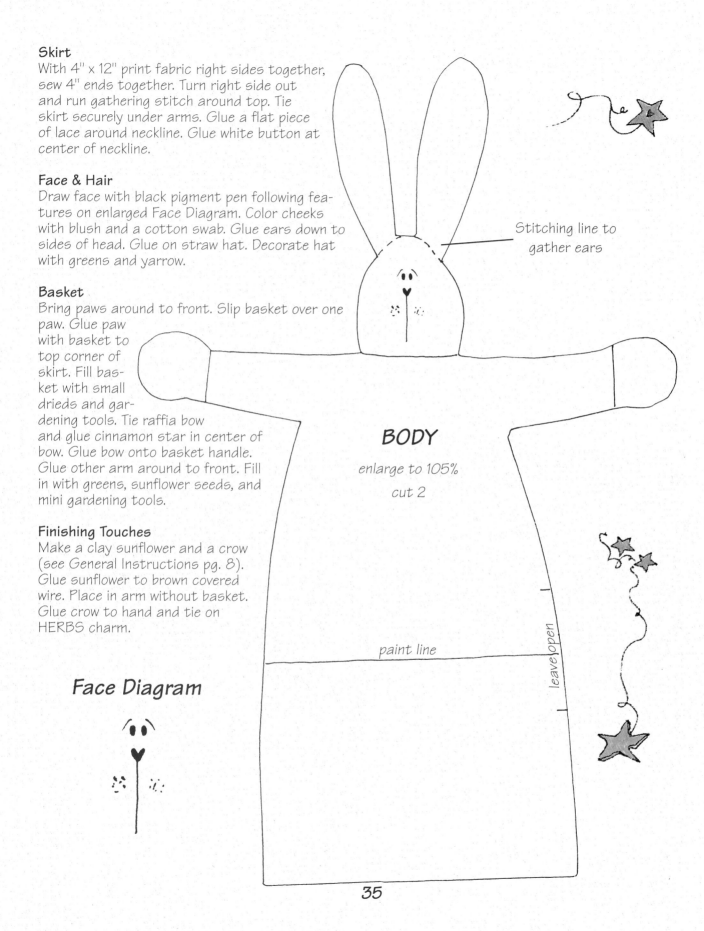

Skirt

With 4" x 12" print fabric right sides together, sew 4" ends together. Turn right side out and run gathering stitch around top. Tie skirt securely under arms. Glue a flat piece of lace around neckline. Glue white button at center of neckline.

Face & Hair

Draw face with black pigment pen following features on enlarged Face Diagram. Color cheeks with blush and a cotton swab. Glue ears down to sides of head. Glue on straw hat. Decorate hat with greens and yarrow.

Basket

Bring paws around to front. Slip basket over one paw. Glue paw with basket to top corner of skirt. Fill basket with small drieds and gardening tools. Tie raffia bow and glue cinnamon star in center of bow. Glue bow onto basket handle. Glue other arm around to front. Fill in with greens, sunflower seeds, and mini gardening tools.

Finishing Touches

Make a clay sunflower and a crow (see General Instructions pg. 8). Glue sunflower to brown covered wire. Place in arm without basket. Glue crow to hand and tie on HERBS charm.

Face Diagram

Stitching line to gather ears

BODY

enlarge to 105%

cut 2

paint line

leave open

35

SNOW DAYS

Materials

Felt: black, scrap (skates)
Flannel or pieced homespun: ¼ yd.
Knit ribbing: scrap (hat)
Muslin: ½ yd. (body)
Plaid: ⅛ yd. (pants)
Wool fabric: 2½" x 12" (scarf)
Batting: all-wool, ¼ yd
Buttons: small (2); bright colored,
    medium, (8-10)
Needle: hand-stitching
Stuffing
Thread: carpet; coordinating
Charm: tin star: ½"
Doily: lace, round, 8"
Jingle bell: large
Wool roving: scrap, grey (hair)
Pigment pen: black, .01; red, .01
Transfer tools
Hot glue gun and glue sticks
Scissors
Sewing machine
Cotton swabs
Paper clips: 2
Powdered blush

Read all instructions before beginning.

Body

Trace around body, leg, and arm patterns (see pg. 41) on doubled piece of muslin. Sew on line. Cut out and turn right side out. Stuff arms to within 1" of end. Stuff legs to 1" of top. Stuff head and body to within 2" of bottom of body. Insert legs into body with toes pointing forward. Stitch across bottom of body and across legs. Make a running stitch across top of arms. Draw up tightly and attach to shoulders.

Coat

Trace around coat pattern (see pg. 40). Cut coat out of flannel or pieced homespun. Split one piece down front along fold. Sew right sides together at shoulder seams. Open out flat. Cut 2 sleeves 3" x 2" out of same fabric. Fit 3" side along shoulder edge and stitch. Cut batting 2" x 24" long. Fold in half to 1" wide, and stitch onto outside cuffs of sleeves. Sew underarm seam by starting at cuff and moving down side of coat. Stitch another strip of batting along bottom of coat. Turn one edge of the front of coat under ½", including the batting, and stitch down front to give coat a finished edge.

Pants

Cut pants out of plaid and sew along seam line. Turn right side out. Run gathering stitches around waist and legs at lines shown on pattern, turning under raw edges ½".

Dressing

Put pants on doll, draw up gathering stitches so pants fit snugly. Put coat on doll, pulling finished side over unfinished. Glue into place. Glue or stitch bright colored medium buttons down front.

shoulder seam

COAT

cut 2 on the fold

fold

fold down for waist

PANTS

cut 2 on the fold

fold

Face & Hair

Draw on face with black and red pigment pens following features on body pattern. Color cheeks with blush and a cotton swab. Sew grey wool on top of head. Let wool peek out under hat.

Wings

Fold 8" lace doily in half and make a finger crease down center. Open doily back up and make a running stitch from one side to the other along crease. Draw up as tightly as possible and stitch to secure. Glue wings to back of coat.

Scarf & Hat

Fold 2½" x 12" wool in half and tie off to one side of neck. Fringe ends. Cut a piece of knit ribbing 4" x 2". Fold in half. Stitch a seam along 2" end. Make a running-stitch across top and draw up tightly. Turn right side out. Fit down over hair and glue in place. Glue bell on top to finish.

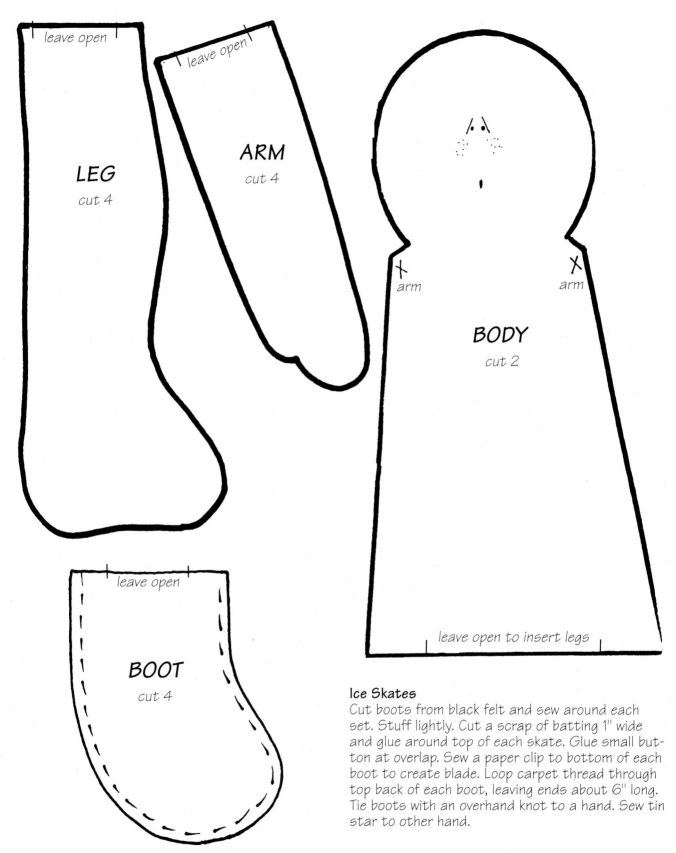

LEG
cut 4

leave open

ARM
cut 4

leave open

arm   arm

BODY
cut 2

leave open to insert legs

BOOT
cut 4

leave open

Ice Skates

Cut boots from black felt and sew around each set. Stuff lightly. Cut a scrap of batting 1" wide and glue around top of each skate. Glue small button at overlap. Sew a paper clip to bottom of each boot to create blade. Loop carpet thread through top back of each boot, leaving ends about 6" long. Tie boots with an overhand knot to a hand. Sew tin star to other hand.

41

Noel Christmas Angel

Materials

Flannel: ⅓ yd. (skirt)
Homespun: ⅓ yd. (band)
Muslin: tea-dyed, ⅓ yd. (body)
Ribbon: chiffon, wired 1" wide, ½ yd.
Button: flower pot
Floss: green; red; yellow
Needles: embroidery; hand-stitching
Stuffing
Thread: carpet; white
Charm: small heart
Doilies: crocheted, round, 4"; lace,
          round, 8"
Greenery: 6"
Holly sprig
Wavy wool braid: blonde, 3"
Wire star
Disappearing transfer pen
Pigment pen: black, .01; red, .01
Transfer tools
Hot glue gun and glue sticks
Iron and ironing board
Scissors
Sewing machine
Cotton swabs
Powdered blush

Read all instructions before beginning.

Body

Trace around body, leg, and arm patterns (see pg. 44) on doubled piece of muslin. Sew on line. Cut out and turn right side out. Stuff arms to within 1" of end. Stuff legs to within 1" of top. Stuff head and body to within 2" of bottom of body. Insert legs into body with toes pointing forward. Stitch across bottom of body and across legs. Make a running stitch across top of arms. Draw up tightly and attach to shoulders.

Dress

Trace around bodice pattern (see pg. 44). Cut bodice out of flannel. Sew along seam lines on pattern. Turn under neck and sleeve edges. Run a gathering stitch with carpet thread along neckline and on each sleeve edge. Put top on doll and draw up thread. Knot off and tie in a bow. Cut one 4" x 22" piece of flannel for skirt. Cut one 4" X 22" piece of contrasting homespun for band. Fold band in half with wrong sides together. Stitch to flannel skirt. Press seam up and topstitch on flannel. With right sides together, stitch center back seam. Turn under top edge ¼" and run a gathering stitch along top of skirt. Draw up tightly around waist, over bodice. Tie off tightly.

43

Skirt Tree

Using disappearing transfer pen, copy Christmas Tree Diagram on front of skirt. Using floss, embroider tree following diagram's stitch instructions. Stitch tiny flower pot button at base of tree.

Collar

Cut a 2½" slit in center of 4" crocheted doily. Pull over head, tucking under stray ends. Tie small heart charm around neck with carpet thread and tie off in a bow.

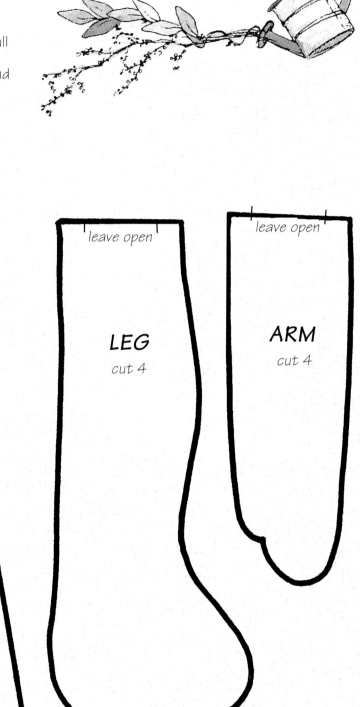

arm

arm

BODY

cut 2

leave open to insert legs

leave open

LEG

cut 4

leave open

ARM

cut 4

Face & Hair

Draw face with black and red pigment pens following features on body pattern. Color cheeks with blush and a cotton swab. Sew blonde wavy wool braid on top of head. Pull apart braid to fluff out.

Wings

Fold 8" lace doily in half and make a finger crease down center. Open doily back up and make a running stitch from one side to the other along crease. Draw up as tightly as possible and stitch to secure. Glue to center back of angel.

Finishing Touches

Form 6" piece of greenery into a circle. Twist ends to hold together. Glue to back of head for halo. Glue a holly sprig to front of halo. Sew wire star to one hand.

Christmas Tree Diagram

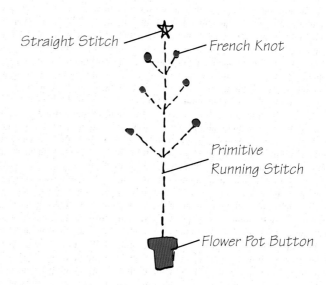

Straight Stitch

French Knot

Primitive Running Stitch

Flower Pot Button

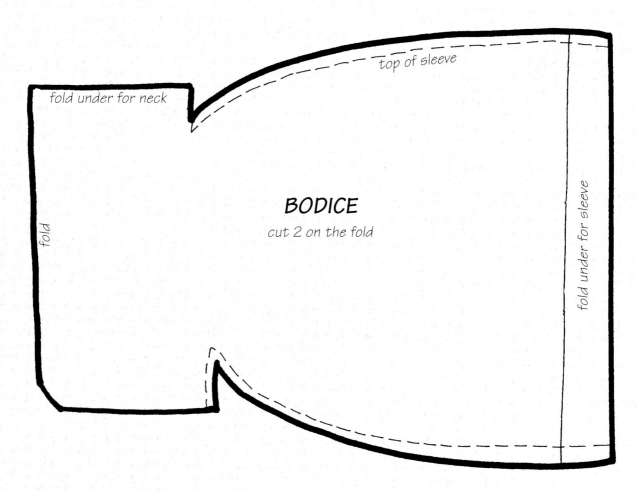

fold under for neck

top of sleeve

fold

fold under for sleeve

BODICE

cut 2 on the fold

Kringle

Materials

Fabric scraps: ginger; green; red
Homespun: scrap, tan (bag)
Muslin: tea-dyed, ½ yd. (body)
Jute
Yarn: thick lumpy wool, ivory, 36"
Needle: hand-stitching
Stuffing
Thread: carpet; cotton
Bell: large, brass
Cinnamon sticks: 6" (2)
Jingle bells: tiny, 2
Miniatures: candy canes (3);
        cinnamon boy, 3";
        cinnamon stars 1", ½"; pine
        cones 6-8; tin candle holder
        with candle; wood mason jar
Preserved: pine; boxwood; holly
Spanish moss
Tansy or yarrow
Wool roving: grey (curly beard)
Paint: blue; med. brown; deep red;
        rose; white
Matte acrylic spray
Pigment pen: black, .01
Transfer tools
Toothpicks
Oven-bake clay: white
Hot glue gun and glue sticks
Iron and ironing board
Paintbrush
Scissors
Sewing machine
Cotton swabs
Kitty litter: 2 cups
Newspaper
Powdered blush

Read all instructions before beginning.

Body
Enlarge body pattern (see pg. 49). Trace around body, arm and hat patterns (see pg. 49) on doubled piece of tea-dyed muslin. Sew on line leaving openings where indicated. Cut out and make a paper bag bottom (see General Instructions pg. 8). Turn right side out. Fill bottom with kitty litter then stuff firmly. Stuff arms and hands firmly. Hand-stitch openings closed.

Hat
With right sides together, stitch hat along seam lines. Turn right side out and stuff with wadded-up newspaper. This makes it easier to paint.

Finish Body
With deep red, paint body to neckline, paint arm to hand line, and paint hat entirely. Let dry. Spray very lightly with a matte acrylic spray. Glue each arm onto back of Kringle (the bag on his back will cover this later). Glue loopy yarn to front of body from the neckline all the way down the front; tuck under at bottom. Glue pieces of yarn around each wrist. Bring hands together in front and cross one over the other. Secure with glue.

Bag
Trace around bag pattern. With right sides together, stitch on traced line on pattern. Leave top open as indicated. Turn right side out and fold top edge under. Press. Fill bag with cinnamon boy, greens, candy canes, and a cinnamon star glued to end of a cinnamon stick. Glue each item in securely (keeping bag somewhat flat works well). Position bag on one back shoulder of Kringle and secure with glue. Allow contents of bag to peek out over shoulder. Tie a piece of jute around Kringle—under one arm, starting and stopping on front of the sack. Tie off in a bow.

Face & Hair
Draw face with black pigment pen following features on enlarged Face Diagram (see pg. 49). Color cheeks with blush and a cotton swab. Glue a small

---

BAG

cut 2

leave open

---

amount of grey wool roving along top of head. After hat is dry, remove newspaper and fold point end over. Glue on a large brass bell. Glue hat onto head exposing some grey hair. Glue a piece of loopy yarn around base of hat.

Gingerbread Boy
Roll oven-bake clay into long skinny "snakes." For each boy, cut 2 pieces ½" long. Roll a small ball for head. Bend the 2 long pieces into "L" shapes. Turn upside down and squish together. Smooth over center seam. Press head on. Bake according to manufacturer's instructions. When cool, paint med. brown. With black paint and point of a toothpick, dot eyes, mouth, and buttons down front of body.

Finishing Touches
Fill arms with pine, boxwood, holly, a cinnamon stick with a cinnamon star on the end, cinnamon boy, and a mini gingerbread man. Tuck Spanish moss and pine cones around hands. Glue cinnamon sticks, candle holder with candle, and wood mason jar to top of hands. Tie homespun scrap in a bow. Glue button on top of bow. With greenery under bow, glue to front of hands.

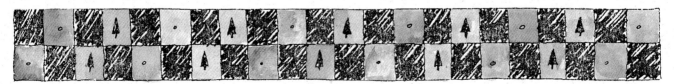

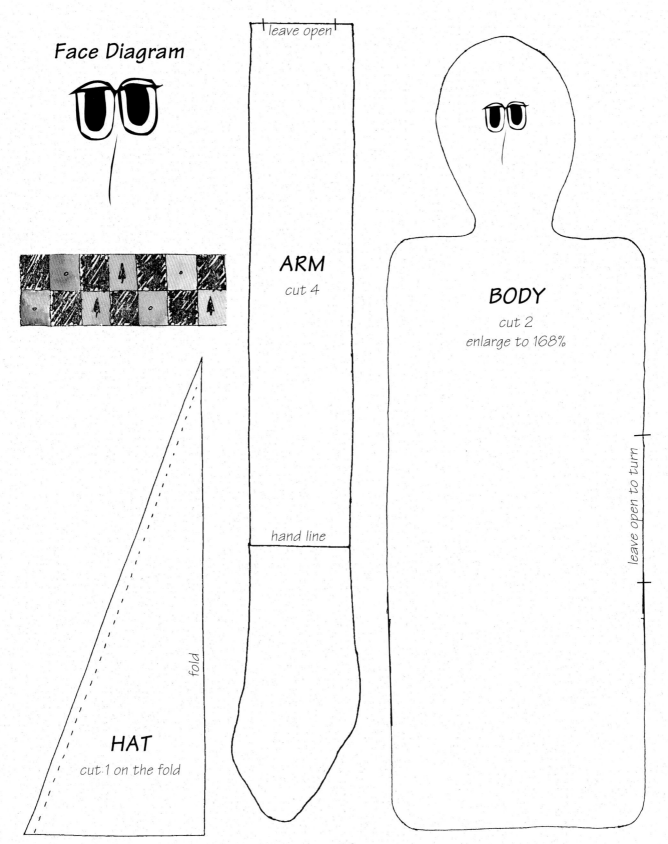

Face Diagram

ARM
cut 4

leave open

hand line

BODY
cut 2
enlarge to 168%

leave open to turn

HAT
cut 1 on the fold

fold

49

Snowlady

Materials

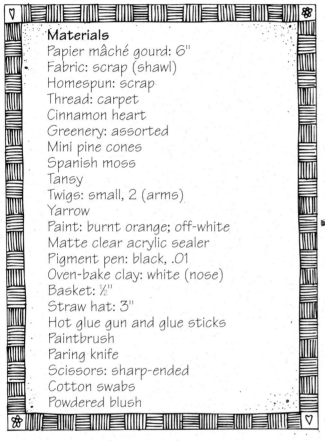

- Papier mâché gourd: 6"
- Fabric: scrap (shawl)
- Homespun: scrap
- Thread: carpet
- Cinnamon heart
- Greenery: assorted
- Mini pine cones
- Spanish moss
- Tansy
- Twigs: small, 2 (arms)
- Yarrow
- Paint: burnt orange; off-white
- Matte clear acrylic sealer
- Pigment pen: black, .01
- Oven-bake clay: white (nose)
- Basket: ½"
- Straw hat: 3"
- Hot glue gun and glue sticks
- Paintbrush
- Paring knife
- Scissors: sharp-ended
- Cotton swabs
- Powdered blush

Read all instructions before beginning.

Body

For best results, use a 6" papier mâché gourd (sometimes called duckpins). Paint entire gourd off-white. Spray lightly with matte clear acrylic sealer. Let dry. Make a hole on two sides of gourd with sharp end of scissors. Cut 2 twigs 4½" long. Put a drop of glue on each twig and insert in holes.

Face

Draw face with black pigment pen. Color cheeks with blush and a cotton swab. Make nose by rolling a small amount of oven-bake clay into a "snake" shape (¼" diameter and 1" long). Roll one end to a blunt point and flatten other end. Cut off ⅝" from point. Make random lines with a paring knife along sides of nose. Bake according to manufacturer's instructions. Let cool. Paint burnt orange. Glue to face. Spray entire face lightly with matte clear acrylic sealer.

Shawl & Hat

Cut triangle from scrap for shawl. Tie on and secure with glue. Decorate hat with Spanish moss, yarrow, greenery, a small piece of homespun, and mini pine cones. Glue hat on tilting back.

Finishing Touches

Tie basket to arm with carpet thread. Glue cinnamon heart at neck.

PEARL THE GOURD ANGEL

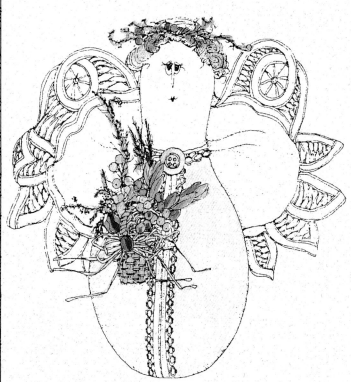

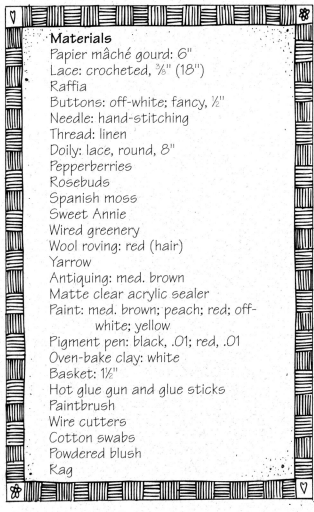

Materials
Papier mâché gourd: 6"
Lace: crocheted, ⅜" (18")
Raffia
Buttons: off-white; fancy, ½"
Needle: hand-stitching
Thread: linen
Doily: lace, round, 8"
Pepperberries
Rosebuds
Spanish moss
Sweet Annie
Wired greenery
Wool roving: red (hair)
Yarrow
Antiquing: med. brown
Matte clear acrylic sealer
Paint: med. brown; peach; red; off-
         white; yellow
Pigment pen: black, .01; red, .01
Oven-bake clay: white
Basket: 1½"
Hot glue gun and glue sticks
Paintbrush
Wire cutters
Cotton swabs
Powdered blush
Rag

Read all instructions before beginning.

For best results, use a papier mâché gourd (sometimes called duckpins). If one is not available, a pattern to make a similar soft body out of muslin is included (see pg. 53).

Body
Paint gourd off-white from neck down. Paint head peach. Spray lightly with matte clear acrylic sealer.

Let dry. Antique gourd with med. brown. Wipe off evenly with rag. After gourd dries, spray another light coat of clear acrylic to seal.

Face & Hair
Draw face with black and red pigment pens following features on body pattern. Color cheeks with blush and a cotton swab. Fluff out wool roving and tie in center with linen thread. Glue on top of head.

Halo
Wrap wired greenery around a 2 oz. paint jar, making a circle that is about 2½" in diameter. Twist ends around each other to close circle and cut off with wire cutters. Glue on back of head. Decorate halo with sprigs of sweet Annie and pepperberries.

Dress

Glue two long pieces of lace down front of doll. Glue another piece of lace around neck; overlap in back. Glue off-white button to center front of neckline.

Wings

Fold 8" lace doily in half and make a finger crease down center. Open doily back up and make a running stitch from one side to the other along crease. Draw up as tightly as possible and stitch to secure. Glue to back of doll.

Basket

Make robin (see General Instructions pg. 8). Fill basket with greens, and decorate with pepperberries, yarrow, rosebuds, robin, and a raffia bow. Glue fancy button to front of basket.

Cloth Body (optional)

Materials

Muslin: ½ yd.
Needle: hand-stitching
Stuffing
Thread: coordinating
Transfer tools
Scissors
Sewing machine
Kitty litter: 1 cup

Instructions

If making a cloth body rather than using a duckpin, trace body pattern on doubled piece of muslin. Sew on line, leaving an opening where indicated. Cut out. Bring side and bottom seams together. Make a paper bag bottom (see General Instructions pg. 8). Turn right side out and fill with kitty litter. Stuff firmly. Hand-stitch opening closed. Paint body off-white. Leave head muslin colored. Follow remaining instructions for Pearl.

CLOTH BODY

(optional)
cut 2

leave open

GRACE

Materials

Flannel: ½ yd. (body)
Homespun: red, scrap
Quilt scrap: 2" x 20" (shawl)
Raffia
Buttons: assorted, ¾" to 1" (8)
Needle: hand-stitching
Stuffing
Thread: coordinating
Cinnamon star: small
Miniatures: hat; seed packets;
        spade; trowel; water can
Sweet Annie: (hair)
Twigs: 6" long (2) (arms)
Paint: burnt orange
Pigment pen: black; .01
Transfer tools
Oven-bake clay: white (nose)
Basket: ½"
Hot glue gun and glue sticks
Paintbrush: fine tip
Paring knife
Scissors
Sewing machine
Cotton swabs
Kitty litter: 1 cup
Powdered blush

Read all instructions before beginning.

Body
Enlarge body pattern (see pg. 56). Trace body on wrong side of doubled flannel. Sew on line, leaving an opening where indicated. Cut out and make a paper bag bottom (see General Instructions pg. 8). Turn right side out. Fill bottom with kitty litter then stuff firmly. Plop her down on a flat surface to make certain she can stand. Hand-stitch opening closed.

Make small slit on each side of doll for arms. Cut 2 twigs and insert into slits with a drop of glue each.

Face & Hair
Draw face with black pigment pen following features on body pattern. Color cheeks with blush and a cotton swab. Group a bit of sweet Annie for hair. Tie a little homespun bow around greens and glue small cinnamon star in center of bow. Glue to top of head.

Nose

Roll a small amount of oven-bake clay into a "snake" shape (about ¼" diameter and 1" long). Roll one end to a blunt point and flatten the other end. Cut off ⅝" from point. Make random lines with a paring knife along sides of nose. Bake according to manufacturer's instructions. Let cool. Paint burnt orange. Glue to face.

Basket

Fill basket with miniatures. Tie basket to twig arm using raffia. A bird's nest or hanging tin stars could be substituted for basket.

Finishing Touches

Glue or tie on assorted buttons down front of body. Fold down edge of 2" X 20" quilt scrap. Fold around neck to look like a scarf. Glue button in center.

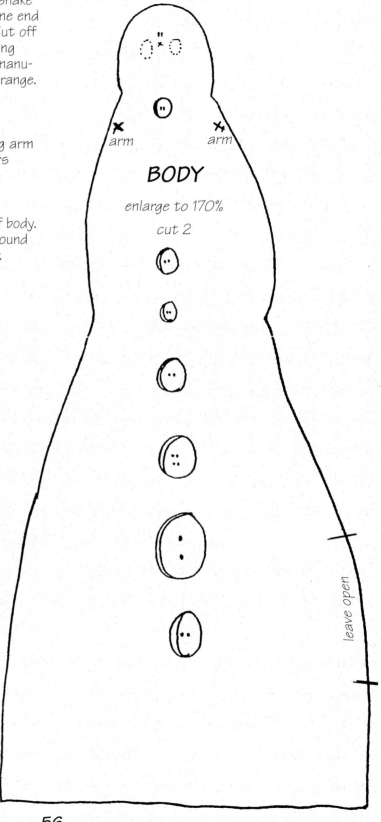

56

Mrs. Gingerbread

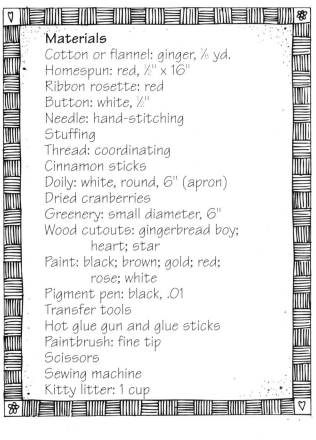

Materials
Cotton or flannel: ginger, ⅛ yd.
Homespun: red, ½" x 16"
Ribbon rosette: red
Button: white, ½"
Needle: hand-stitching
Stuffing
Thread: coordinating
Cinnamon sticks
Doily: white, round, 6" (apron)
Dried cranberries
Greenery: small diameter, 6"
Wood cutouts: gingerbread boy;
      heart; star
Paint: black; brown; gold; red;
      rose; white
Pigment pen: black, .01
Transfer tools
Hot glue gun and glue sticks
Paintbrush: fine tip
Scissors
Sewing machine
Kitty litter: 1 cup

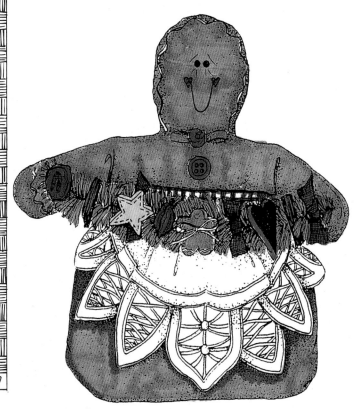

Read all instructions before beginning.

Body
Trace body pattern (see pg. 59) on doubled piece of ginger-colored fabric. Sew on line leaving an opening where indicated. Cut out and make a paper bag bottom (see General Instructions pg. 8). Turn right side out. Fill bottom with kitty litter then stuff firmly. Hand-stitch opening closed.

Apron
Cut 6" doily in half. Stitch a running thread along cut side and pull to gather. Glue in place at waist (see apron line pg. 59). Cut a piece of homespun ½" x 16" for apron waistband. Center across front of apron, glue in place. Tie apron strings in back. Glue red rosette at neck.

Face
Paint face following features on body pattern. Paint rose-colored hearts for cheeks. Using handle end of paintbrush, dot eyes with black paint. Let dry. Use black pigment pen to add expression to mouth and eyes.

58

Garland

Tie three knotted strips of homespun on 6" greenery. Glue on cinnamon stick pieces, dried cranberries, and painted wood pieces. Pull arms to front and glue on garland. Hold ends until glue is dry.

Finishing Touches

With white paint and fine tip paintbrush, paint "icing" around head and arms as shown in photograph (see pg.57). Let dry. Paint wood heart red, wood gingerbread boy brown with white "icing," and wood star gold. Let dry. After star is dry, glue small white button on top. Use black pigment pen to draw details on wood pieces.

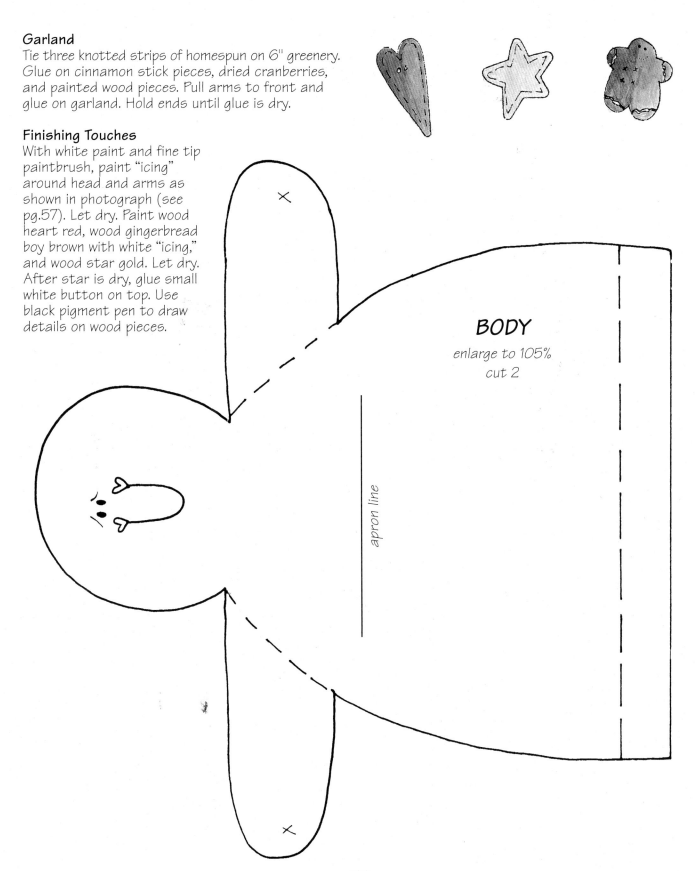

BODY
enlarge to 105%
cut 2

apron line

Christmas Caroler

Materials
Homespun: scrap (scarf)
Muslin: tea-dyed, ¼ yd. (body)
Batting: natural
Needle: hand-stitching
Stuffing
Thread: carpet; coordinating
Yarn: wool, loopy, scrap
Bell: small
Miniature: candle holder with candle
Paint: black; green; red
Pigment pens: black, .01; red, .01
Transfer tools
Hot glue gun and glue sticks
Paintbrush: fine tip
Scissors
Sewing machine
Cardstock: heavy
Cotton swabs
Powdered blush

Read all instructions before beginning.

Body
Trace body pattern (see pg. 61) on doubled piece of tea-dyed muslin. Sew on line, leaving an opening where indicated. Cut ⅛" outside stitching, clipping curves and corners. Turn right side out. Stuff hands. Leave arms unstuffed. Firmly stuff body, head, and legs. Hand-stitch opening closed.

Paint

Paint legs black. Let dry. Use Diagram 1 to outline face on body. Paint "coat" green, leaving face peeking out. Paint mittens red. Let dry.

Coat

Cut a strip of natural batting ½" x 24". Wrap around bottom of coat, leaving one edge even with bottom of coat. Glue securely, beginning and ending in back. Glue another strip of batting down center front of coat, beginning under chin.

Face & Hair

Draw face with black and red pigment pens following enlarged features in Diagram 2. Color cheeks with blush and a cotton swab. Glue loopy wool yarn around face and cuffs.

Sheet Music

Photocopy music pattern onto heavy cardstock. Bring arms to front and glue hands together. Place sheet music in hands and glue candle and holder in outer hand. It should appear that caroler is reading music by candlelight.

Finishing Touches

Cut 1" x 8" strip of wool for scarf and tie around neck. Glue bell to top of hat. Tie carpet thread to top of head to hang her. Make a whole group of ornaments in various colors to complete the choir!!

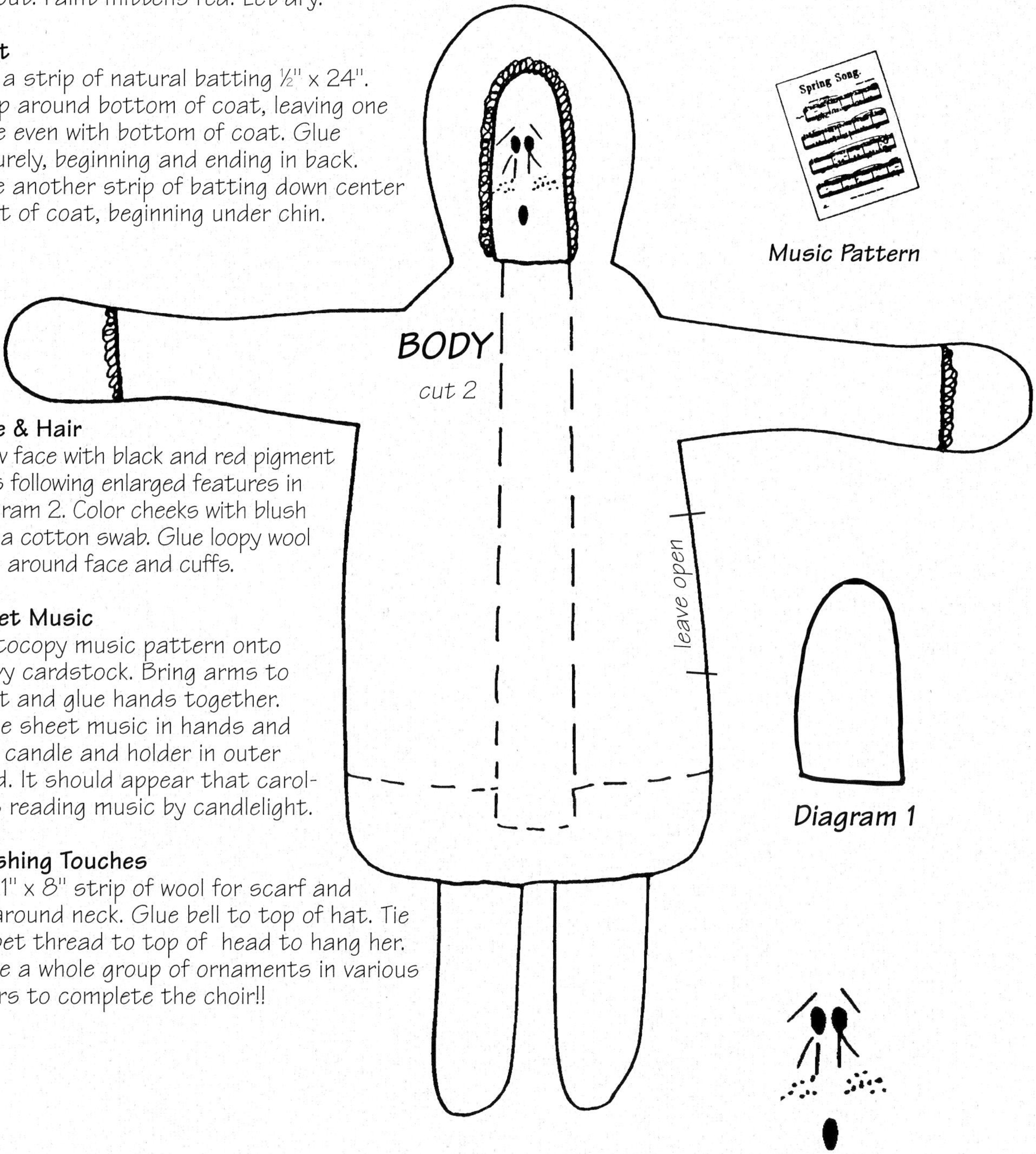

BODY

cut 2

leave open

Music Pattern

Spring Song

Diagram 1

Diagram 2

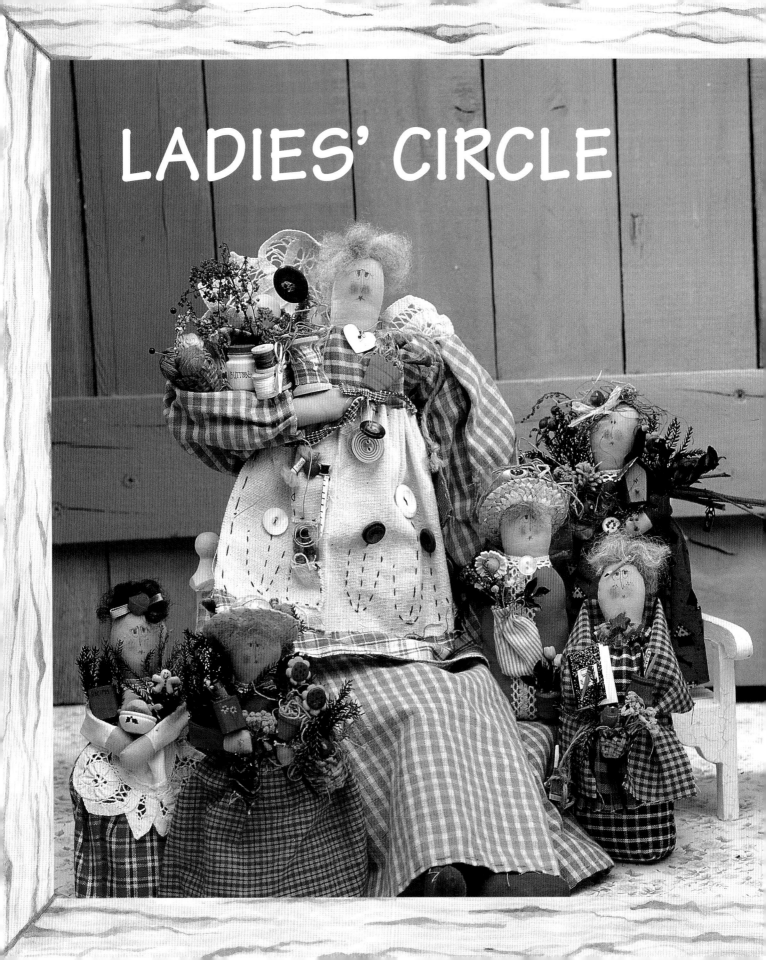

LADIES' CIRCLE

Beatrice

Materials

Homespun: plaid, ½ yd.
Muslin: ½ yd. (body)
Jute
Buttons: antique, large, 2 or 3
Needle: hand-stitching
Straight pins
Stuffing
Thread: carpet; coordinating
Charm: tin heart
Doily: white, crocheted, round, 4"
Greens: various
Miniatures: birdhouse, 3"; flower
        pot, 1"; mason jars (3);
        shovel; wood sunflowers (2)
Pepperberries: red
Spanish moss
Tansy
Wool hair: dk. brown, small piece
Paint: black; dk. brown; gold; green;
        mustard; barn red; white
Pigment pens: black, .01; red, .01
Transfer tools
Twigs
Wire: covered
Oven-bake clay: white
Basket: 2-3" (papier mâché)
Straw hat: 3"
Hot glue gun and glue sticks
Iron and ironing board
Paintbrush: fine tip
Scissors
Sewing machine
Cotton swabs
Kitty litter: 1 cup
Powdered blush

Read all instructions before beginning.

Body
Enlarge body pattern (see pg. 67). Trace around body and hand patterns (see pgs. 66- 67) on doubled piece of muslin. Sew on line. Cut out and turn right side out. Stuff hands firmly. Cut body piece out and make paper bag bottom (see General Instructions on pg. 8). Turn right side out. Fill bottom with kitty litter then stuff firmly. Hand-stitch opening closed.

Dress
Trace around bodice pattern. Cut bodice, 2 sleeves 6½"x 8", and 2 skirts 11½" x 14" out of plaid homespun. Gather top of sleeve to fit bodice and pin in place. Gather and pin skirts onto front and back of bodice. With right sides together, sew underarm and side seams. Clip under arms and turn right side out. Press sleeve edges under ½" and gather with carpet thread. Gather stitch around neck opening. Pull neck opening over head. Draw up neckline around neck and tie off at front. Gather seams around hands. Put a few drops of glue under stitching to secure. Tie off thread in a bow.

Collar
Cut a 2½" slit in center of 4" crocheted doily. Pull over head, tucking under stray ends. Tie tin heart around neck with carpet thread and tie off in a bow.

Face & Hair
Draw face with black and red pigment pens following enlarged features in Diagram 4. Color cheeks using blush and a cotton swab. Glue a small amount of wool hair to top of head.

Accessories
Paint and detail wood sunflowers, birdhouse, and mason jars (see Diagrams 1-3). Paint flowerpot as desired. Let dry. Make a clay sunflower and crow (see General Instructions pg. 8).

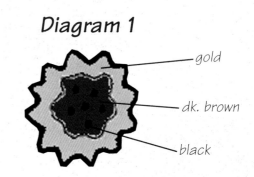

Diagram 1

gold

dk. brown

black

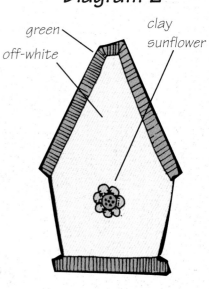

HAND
cut 4

leave open

Diagram 2

green

off-white

clay
sunflower

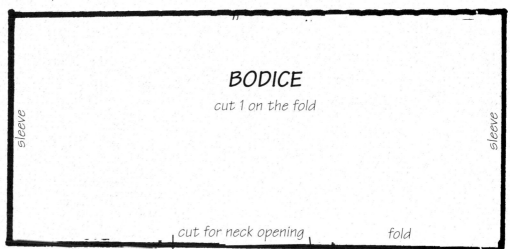

BODICE
cut 1 on the fold

sleeve

sleeve

cut for neck opening

fold

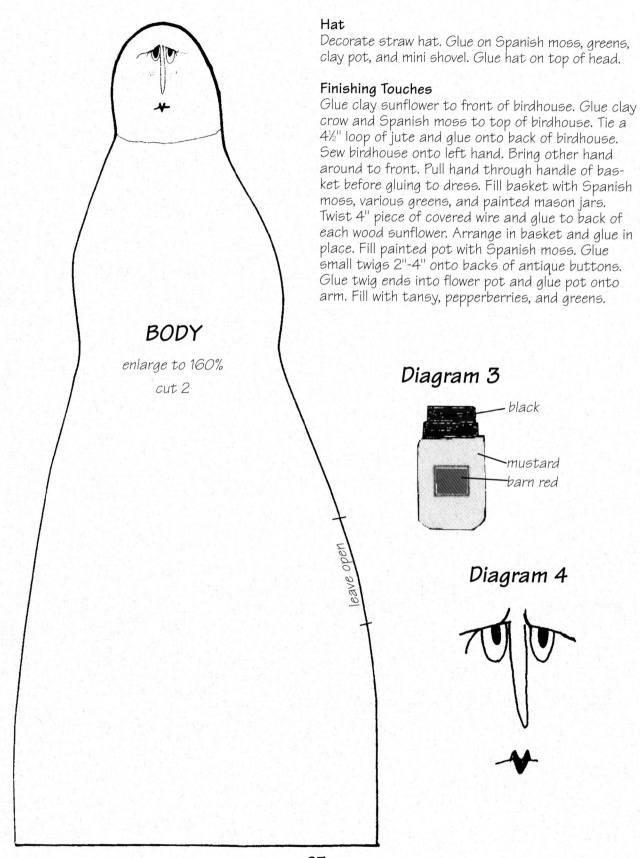

Hat

Decorate straw hat. Glue on Spanish moss, greens, clay pot, and mini shovel. Glue hat on top of head.

Finishing Touches

Glue clay sunflower to front of birdhouse. Glue clay crow and Spanish moss to top of birdhouse. Tie a 4½" loop of jute and glue onto back of birdhouse. Sew birdhouse onto left hand. Bring other hand around to front. Pull hand through handle of basket before gluing to dress. Fill basket with Spanish moss, various greens, and painted mason jars. Twist 4" piece of covered wire and glue to back of each wood sunflower. Arrange in basket and glue in place. Fill painted pot with Spanish moss. Glue small twigs 2"-4" onto backs of antique buttons. Glue twig ends into flower pot and glue pot onto arm. Fill with tansy, pepperberries, and greens.

BODY

enlarge to 160%

cut 2

leave open

Diagram 3

black

mustard

barn red

Diagram 4

67

SADIE

Materials

Homespun: blue, 4" x 12" (skirt)
Muslin: tea-dyed, ⅛ yd. (body)
Lace: flat, ⅜", 1 yd.
Needle: hand-stitching
Stuffing
Thread: coordinating
Boxwood
Cinnamon heart: small
Cinnamon stick: small
Greenery
Miniatures: wood flower pot;
            wood book
Spanish moss
Wool roving: grey (hair)
Paint: brown; red brown; green;
       rust; yellow
Pigment pens: black, .01; red, .01
Transfer tools
Wire: brown
Oven-bake clay: white
Basket: 1"
Straw hat: 2"
Hot glue gun and glue sticks
Paintbrush: fine tip
Scissors
Sewing machine
Cotton swabs
Kitty litter: ½ cup
Powdered blush

Read all instructions before beginning.

Body

Trace body pattern (see pg. 70) on doubled piece of muslin. Sew on line, leaving opening where indicated. Make paper bag bottom (see General Instructions pg. 8). Turn right side out. Fill bottom with kitty litter. Stuff each hand with a small amount of stuffing. Leave arms unstuffed. Stuff body and head firmly. Hand-stitch opening closed. Using rust paint, paint arms (sleeves) and bodice down to paint line (see body pattern pg. 70). Let dry.

69

Skirt

With right sides together, stitch 4" ends of home-spun together. Turn right side out; seam becomes center back. Make a running stitch along one edge, starting and ending on front of skirt. After bodice is dry, tie skirt onto body under arms. Glue flat lace around neckline.

Face & Hair

Draw face with black and red pigment pens following enlarged features in Diagram 1. Color cheeks with blush and a cotton swab. Sew a small amount of grey wool hair to center of head. Pull hair down around face. Glue on straw hat. Decorate hat with greens and a bow made from skirt fabric. Glue cinnamon heart in center of bow.

Accessories

Paint wood book (see Diagram 2). Make a clay sunflower and a robin (see General Instructions pg. 8). Twist a doubled piece of brown wire and glue to clay sunflower. Paint wood flower pot red brown. Fill flower pot with Spanish moss. Put a drop of glue on end of wire and glue sunflower into pot.

Basket

Fill basket with greenery and robin. Put doll's arm through basket handle and glue in place. Glue flower pot onto hand holding basket. Glue book and cinnamon sticks on other hand.

Finishing Touches

String about 20 small leaves from a stem of preserved box-wood for a garland. Stitch onto hand.

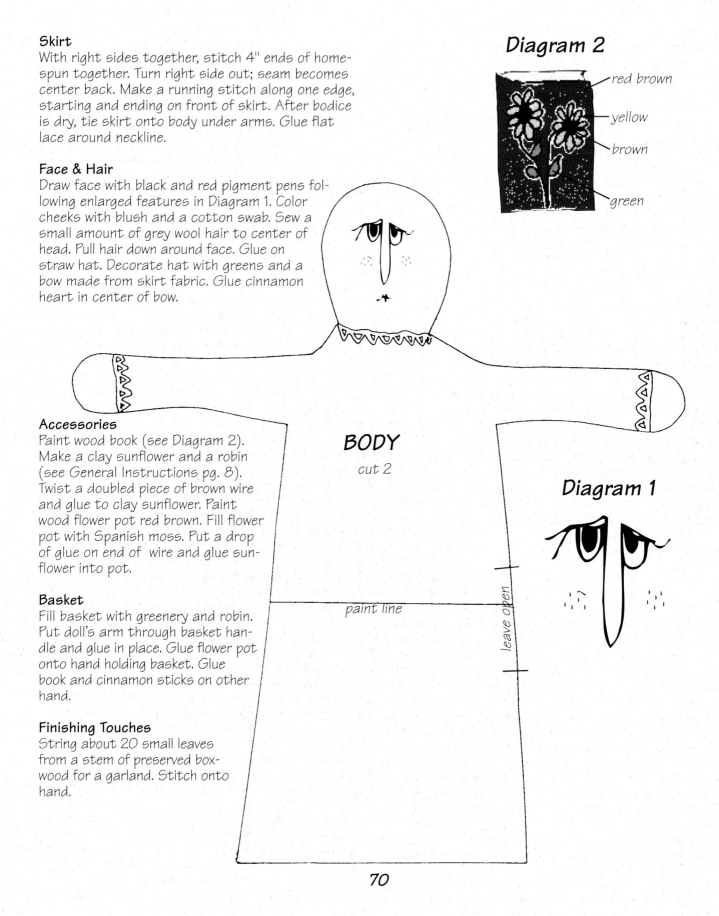

Diagram 2

red brown

yellow

brown

green

BODY

cut 2

paint line

leave open

Diagram 1

EMMA LEA

Materials
Homespun: blue, 4" x 12" (skirt)
Muslin: tea-dyed, ⅛ yd. (body)
Lace: flat, ⅜" wide, 1 yd.
Raffia
Button: antique, small, white
Needle: hand-stitching
Stuffing
Thread: coordinating
Artemisia
Boxwood
Cinnamon star or heart: small
Cinnamon stick: small
Greens and everlastings
Miniatures: mason jar; vegetables;
    wood plate
Princess pine
Spanish moss
Tansy
Wool roving: red (hair)
Paint: black; blue; brown; clay;
    harvest gold; green;
    mustard; off-white
Pigment pens: black, .01; red, .01
Transfer tools
Baskets: ½"; 1"
Hot glue gun and glue sticks
Paintbrush: fine tip
Scissors
Sewing machine
Cotton swabs
Kitty litter
Powdered blush

Read all instructions before beginning.
Emma Lea is photographed twice on pg. 71.

Body
Trace body pattern (see pg. 73) on doubled piece of muslin. Sew on line, leaving an opening where indicated. Cut out and make a paper bag bottom (see General Instructions pg. 8). Turn right side out. Fill bottom with kitty litter. Stuff each hand with a small amount of stuffing; leave arms unstuffed. Stuff body and head firmly. Hand-stitch opening closed. Paint upper body harvest gold, painting to line shown on pattern. Let dry.

72

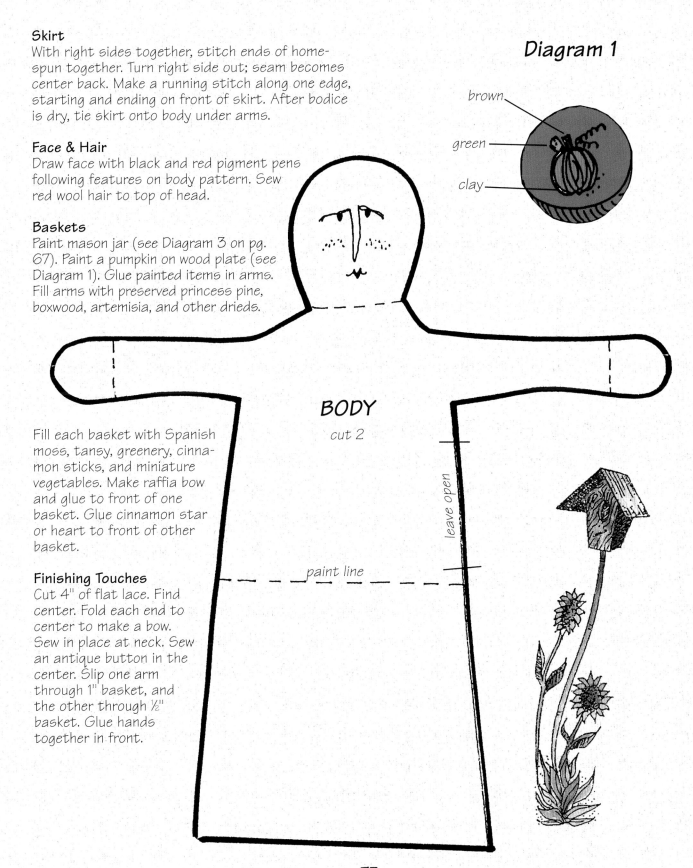

Skirt

With right sides together, stitch ends of home-spun together. Turn right side out; seam becomes center back. Make a running stitch along one edge, starting and ending on front of skirt. After bodice is dry, tie skirt onto body under arms.

Face & Hair

Draw face with black and red pigment pens following features on body pattern. Sew red wool hair to top of head.

Baskets

Paint mason jar (see Diagram 3 on pg. 67). Paint a pumpkin on wood plate (see Diagram 1). Glue painted items in arms. Fill arms with preserved princess pine, boxwood, artemisia, and other drieds.

Fill each basket with Spanish moss, tansy, greenery, cinnamon sticks, and miniature vegetables. Make raffia bow and glue to front of one basket. Glue cinnamon star or heart to front of other basket.

Finishing Touches

Cut 4" of flat lace. Find center. Fold each end to center to make a bow. Sew in place at neck. Sew an antique button in the center. Slip one arm through 1" basket, and the other through ½" basket. Glue hands together in front.

Diagram 1

brown

green

clay

BODY

cut 2

leave open

paint line

Margaret
The Sewing Angel

Materials

Fabrics: contrasting, 4" x 12"; blue,
    woven scrap
Flannel: white, heavy (optional)
Homespun: ⅓ yd. (dress)
Muslin: tea-dyed, ½ yd. (body)
Osnaburg: scrap
Batting (optional)
Floss: 4 colors
Jute
Straight pins: ball head; steel head
Needles: embroidery; hand-stitching
Thread: carpet; coordinating
Wool roving: grey, 3"
Beads: 4
Buttons: assorted, 20
Charm: tin heart
Doily: lace, round, 8" (wings)
Greenery
Miniatures: ; birdhouse with bird;
    flower pot, ½"; scissors; wood
    mason jar; spools, ½" (3); 1" (1)
Spanish moss
Paint: blue; red brown; green; white
Disappearing transfer pen
Pigment pens: black, .01; red, .01
Transfer tools
Oven-bake clay: red
Basket: 1"
Hot glue gun and glue stick
Iron and ironing board
Scissors
Sewing machine
Paintbrush: fine tip
Cotton swabs
Paper: heavy, white
Powdered blush

Button Card
Cut heavy white paper into small rectangle. Using black pigment pen, write BUTTONS at top of card. Glue four small beads in a square underneath (see Diagram 1).

Mason Jar
Paint wood jar white with a rose colored lid. Using black pigment pen, write BUTTONS on side (see Diagram 2).

Necklace Garland
String a small piece of homespun with 10 buttons of various sizes and colors. Sew onto hand that is glued to front. Tie a bow out of homespun and glue to hand at top of button garland.

Pin Cushion
Roll a piece of red oven-bake clay into ball (about ¼" in diameter). Stick three steel head pins in ball away from center. Bake clay according to manufacturer's instructions. When cool, paint a green star on top (see Diagram 3).

Spool
Wrap a strip of homespun around wood spool. Thread greenery through holes of a button. Make about 3" stem, then bend extra wire around in a rounded leaf shape. Glue base into spool. Fill in base with a small amount of Spanish moss.

Thread
Wrap three colors of floss around center of three ½" spools. Glue together in a triangle shape.

Yarn Balls
Wrap three colors of floss in balls about ¾" diameter. Glue into top of 1" basket without a handle. Stick two ball head pins into yarn balls to look like knitting needles.

Finishing Touches
Glue miniature scissors and other accessories in arm that is glued to chest. Herbs and dried greenery work well to fill in spots. Add a clay pot to tip of fingers.

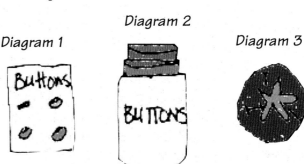

Diagram 1   Diagram 2   Diagram 3

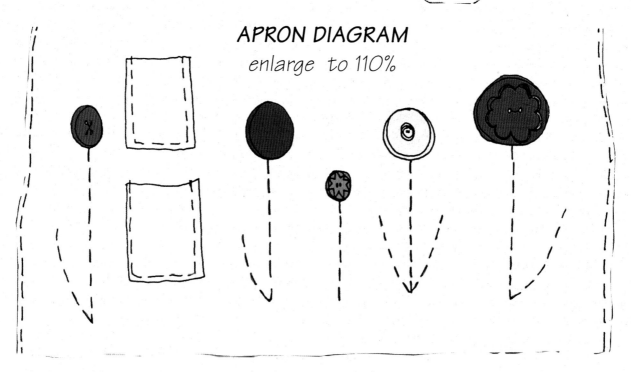

APRON DIAGRAM
enlarge to 110%

78

Maggie

Materials

Fabric: 5" x 12" (skirt)
Muslin: ⅓ yd. (body)
Flat lace: ⅜"
Raffia
Buttons: ⅜" (2)
Needle: hand-stitching
Stuffing
Thread: carpet; coordinating
Miniature: tin birdhouse
Nest: 1"
Rose hips
Sage
Spanish moss (hair)
Sweet Annie
Yarrow
Paint: black; brown; gold; green; red
Pigment pens: black, .01; red, .01
Transfer tools
Balsa: scraps
Toothpicks
Twigs: pieces (wings)
Tin: scrap
Wire: small gauge
Oven-bake clay: white
Craft knife
Hot glue gun and glue sticks
Paintbrush: fine tip
Scissors
Sewing machine
Cotton swabs
Kitty litter: ½ cup
Powdered blush

Read all instructions before beginning.

Body

Trace body pattern (see pg. 81) on doubled piece of muslin. Sew on line, leaving an opening where indicated. Cut out and make a paper bag bottom (see General Instructions pg. 8). Turn right side out. Fill bottom with kitty litter then stuff firmly. Hand-stitch opening closed.

Dress

Paint bodice of doll green; within lines shown on body pattern. Let dry. With right sides together, sew a seam down 5" side of 5" x 12" piece of fabric. Turn right side out and make a running stitch along top with carpet thread. Leave ends long enough to tie. Put skirt on doll and tie tightly. Glue flat lace at neck. Glue buttons down front of bodice.

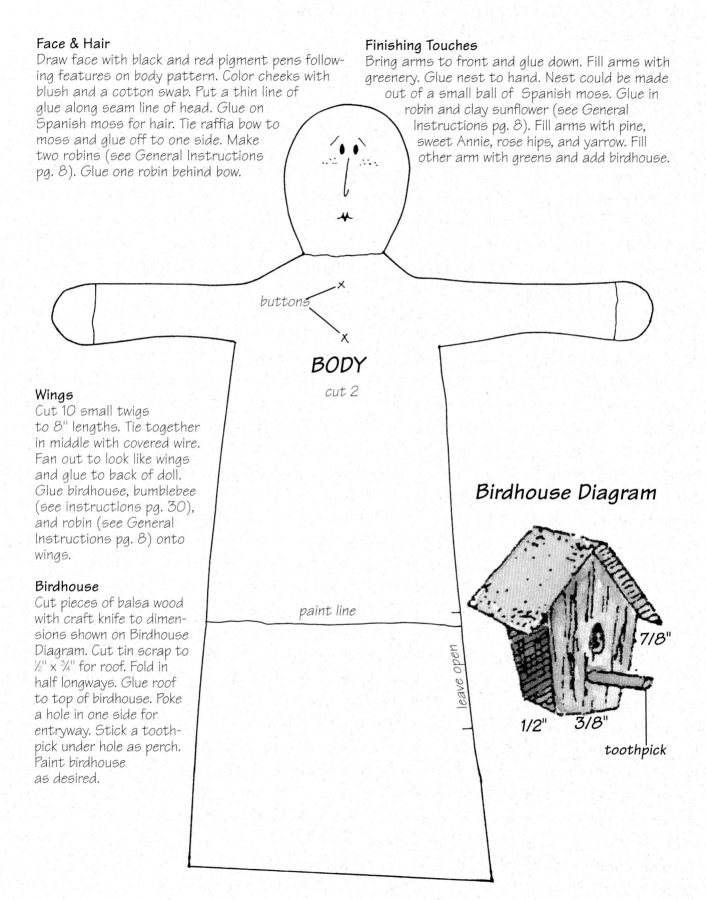

Face & Hair

Draw face with black and red pigment pens following features on body pattern. Color cheeks with blush and a cotton swab. Put a thin line of glue along seam line of head. Glue on Spanish moss for hair. Tie raffia bow to moss and glue off to one side. Make two robins (see General Instructions pg. 8). Glue one robin behind bow.

Finishing Touches

Bring arms to front and glue down. Fill arms with greenery. Glue nest to hand. Nest could be made out of a small ball of Spanish moss. Glue in robin and clay sunflower (see General Instructions pg. 8). Fill arms with pine, sweet Annie, rose hips, and yarrow. Fill other arm with greens and add birdhouse.

buttons

BODY

cut 2

Wings

Cut 10 small twigs to 8" lengths. Tie together in middle with covered wire. Fan out to look like wings and glue to back of doll. Glue birdhouse, bumblebee (see instructions pg. 30), and robin (see General Instructions pg. 8) onto wings.

Birdhouse

Cut pieces of balsa wood with craft knife to dimensions shown on Birdhouse Diagram. Cut tin scrap to ½" x ¾" for roof. Fold in half longways. Glue roof to top of birdhouse. Poke a hole in one side for entryway. Stick a toothpick under hole as perch. Paint birdhouse as desired.

paint line

leave open

Birdhouse Diagram

7/8"

1/2"   3/8"

toothpick

81

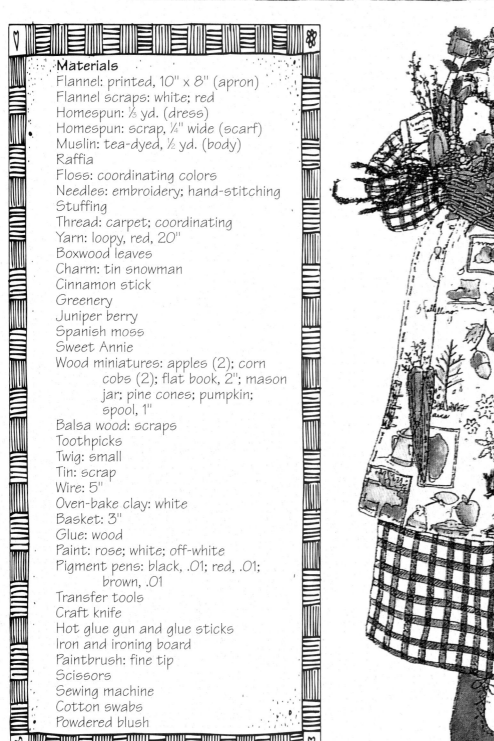

Materials

Flannel: printed, 10" x 8" (apron)
Flannel scraps: white; red
Homespun: ⅓ yd. (dress)
Homespun: scrap, ¼" wide (scarf)
Muslin: tea-dyed, ½ yd. (body)
Raffia
Floss: coordinating colors
Needles: embroidery; hand-stitching
Stuffing
Thread: carpet; coordinating
Yarn: loopy, red, 20"
Boxwood leaves
Charm: tin snowman
Cinnamon stick
Greenery
Juniper berry
Spanish moss
Sweet Annie
Wood miniatures: apples (2); corn
        cobs (2); flat book, 2"; mason
        jar; pine cones; pumpkin;
        spool, 1"
Balsa wood: scraps
Toothpicks
Twig: small
Tin: scrap
Wire: 5"
Oven-bake clay: white
Basket: 3"
Glue: wood
Paint: rose; white; off-white
Pigment pens: black, .01; red, .01;
        brown, .01
Transfer tools
Craft knife
Hot glue gun and glue sticks
Iron and ironing board
Paintbrush: fine tip
Scissors
Sewing machine
Cotton swabs
Powdered blush

Read all instructions before beginning.

Body

Enlarge body, and leg patterns. Trace around body, leg and hand patterns on doubled piece of tea-dyed muslin. Sew on line, leaving openings where indicated. Cut out each piece ⅛" outside seam. Turn right side out. Stuff head and body to within 2" from bottom of body. Stuff hands to within 1" of edge. Stuff legs to within 1" of top. Insert legs into body with toes pointing forward. Stitch across bottom of body and across legs using carpet thread.

Shoes

Paint feet forming shoes. Let dry. Using carpet thread, lace up shoes. Start at base of legs, work up as far as legs are painted. Glue loopy yarn around shoe tops.

Dress

Trace around bodice pattern (see pg. 85). Cut bodice out of homespun. Cut two 14½" x 16" pieces of homespun for skirt. Cut 2 sleeves 6" x 8". Gather 8" side of sleeve and attach to bodice using a ¼" seam allowance. Press seam to inside and repeat with other sleeve. Gather 16" side of each skirt and sew to waist of bodice. With right sides together, sew sleeves and side seams. Clip at under arms. Turn right side out. Press sleeve edge under ½". Make a running stitch around each sleeve. Insert a hand piece and draw up sleeve around it tightly. Knot and tie off ends in bow. Cut bodice between marks for neck opening. Make a running stitch along neck opening; gather to fit around neck. Turn under hem of dress ½" and press. Make a running stitch for hem. Tie dress on doll. Draw up tightly around neck. Tie tin snowman at neck.

Apron

Cut one piece of fabric 10" x 8". Turn under bottom and side edges ¼" and press. Make a primitive running stitch with a contrast piece of floss along each of these edges. Cut out heart pattern (see pg. 85) and hand-stitch to skirt (see photo pg. 82). Turn top edge under ½" and run a long piece of carpet thread through. Tie apron tightly around waist and tie off in a bow.

BODY

enlarge to 125%
cut 2

leave open to insert legs

LEG

enlarge to 125%
cut 4

leave open

Face & Hair

Draw face with black and red pigment pens following features on body pattern. Color cheeks with blush and a cotton swab. Wind a piece of red loopy yarn around 3 fingers three times. Fold in half to find middle and tack onto top of head. Glue a few boxwood leaves and a juniper berry to center.

Basket

Put an arm through 3" basket and glue hand to middle of waistline. Fill basket with Spanish moss, miniature pine cones, pumpkin, corn cobs, apples, and cinnamon sticks.

Prayer Journal & Snowman

Paint flat wood book off-white and antique. Write "to everything there is a season" on front with brown pigment pen and glue on a small raffia bow. Glue book behind basket and fill arm with cinnamon stick, sweet Annie and berries. Make mini snowman (see pg. 96) and place in arms.

Mason Jar

Paint wood jar white with a rose colored lid. Using the black pigment pen write BUTTONS on side (see Diagram 2 on pg. 78).

Birdhouse

See instructions on pg. 81.

Fence

Using craft knife, cut 5 pieces of balsa wood ½" x ¾". Cut three pieces with points at one end for picket fence. Assemble with wood glue (see Fence Diagram). Transfer crow pattern onto balsa wood and cut out one crow. Perch crow on fence in a nest of Spanish moss. Cut a 5" piece of wire and insert one end into bottom of birdhouse, and the other into fence. Paint fence and birdhouse colors that match doll's dress. When dry, put fence on arm of doll. Refer to photograph for positioning (see pg. 82). Make a small wreath out of greenery and tie on a homespun bow. Hang wreath over a picket of fence.

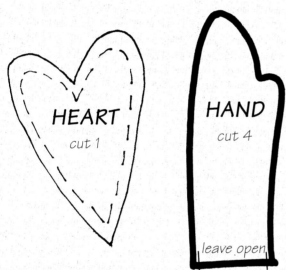

HEART
cut 1

HAND
cut 4

leave open

Fence Diagram

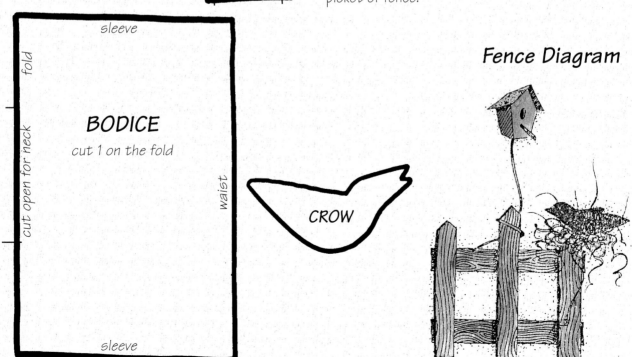

sleeve

fold

BODICE
cut 1 on the fold

cut open for neck

waist

sleeve

CROW

PATSY THE BAKER

Materials

Homespun: red, 4" x 12" (skirt)
Muslin: tea-dyed, ¼ yd. (body)
Ribbon rosette: red
Ribbon: red, ½" (8")
Lace: ⅜" (¼ yd.)
Needle: hand-stitching
Stuffing
Thread: coordinating
Curly braid: brown, 2"
Doily: lace, round, 4" (apron)
Greenery: various
Miniatures: candy cane; cookie
       cutter; rolling pin; wood
       book; wood bowl, ¾"
Paint: med. brown; black; green;
     red; off-white
Pigment pens: black, .01; red, .01
Transfer tools
Oven-bake clay: white
Hot glue gun and glue sticks
Paintbrush: fine tip
Scissors
Sewing machine
Cotton swabs
Kitty litter: ¾ cup
Powdered blush

Read all instructions before beginning.

Body

Trace body pattern (see pg. 88) on doubled piece of muslin. Sew on line, leaving opening where indicated. Cut out and make paper bag bottom (see General Instructions pg. 8). Turn right side out. Fill bottom with kitty litter. Stuff hands. Leave rest of arm unstuffed. Stuff head and body firmly. Hand-stitch opening closed. Paint upper body and arms off-white. Let dry.

Skirt & Apron

With right sides together, sew a seam across 4" ends of 4" x 12" red homespun. Turn right side out and make a gathering stitch around top edge. Tie securely under arms. Cut 4" doily in half and gather across raw edge. Glue apron on doll at waist.

Face & Hair
Draw face with black and red pigment pens following features on body pattern. Color cheeks with blush and a cotton swab. Sew curly braid on top of head. Glue ribbon rosette over stitching.

Recipe Book
Paint wood book red. Let dry. Using black pigment pen, write "RECIPES" across front.

Holly Bowl
Paint small wood bowl off-white. Let dry. Paint small holly leaves and berries on one side (see Diagram 1).

Cookie Dough
Take a small amount of oven-bake clay and roll into a ball. Flatten onto a hard surface and gently push miniature rolling pin down into center of "cookie dough" (see Diagram 2). Bake according to manufacturer's instructions.

Gingerbread Boy
Follow instructions on pg. 48.

Finishing Touches
Glue flat lace around neck. Glue hands together in front. Hot glue cookie dough, holly bowl, mini candy canes, recipe book, and gingerbread boy in arms. Fill in with greenery.

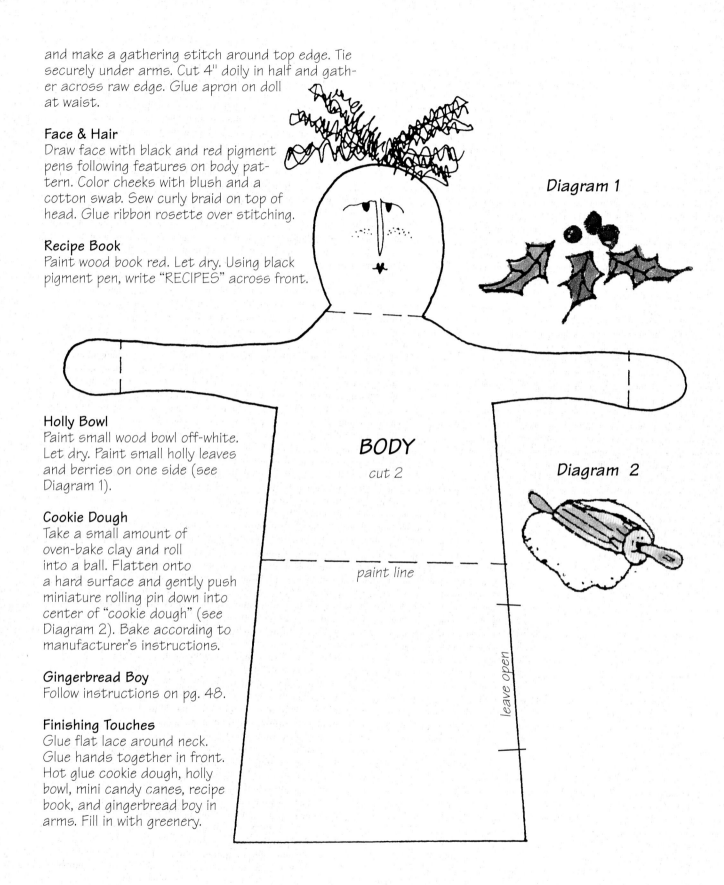

Diagram 1

Diagram 2

BODY

cut 2

paint line

leave open

Miss Elizabeth

Materials

Homespun: ⅛ yd. (apron, shawl)
Homespun: ⅛ yd. (dress)
Muslin: tea-dyed, scrap (body)
Jute: thin
Needle: hand-stitching
Stuffing
Thread: carpet; coordinating
Cinnamon star
Curly braid: grey, 2"
Miniatures: apple; composition
       book; jar; pencils (3);
       ruler; wood books (3)
Spanish moss
Yarrow
Paint: coordinating colors
Pigment pens: black, .01; red, .01
Transfer tools
Basket: 1"
Hot glue gun and glue sticks
Paintbrush: fine tip
Scissors
Sewing machine
Cotton swabs
Kitty litter: ½ cup
Powdered blush

Read all instructions before beginning.

Body

Trace body pattern (see pg. 91) on doubled piece of muslin. Sew on line, leaving opening where indicated. Cut ⅛" outside seam and turn right side out. Stuff firmly. Hand-stitch opening closed.

Dress

Trace dress pattern (see pg. 91) on a doubled piece of homespun. Sew on line, leaving an opening at top. Cut ⅛" outside seam line. Make paper bag bottom (see General Instructions pg. 8). Turn right side out. Fill bottom with kitty litter. Stuff firmly. Turn upper edge down ¼" and make a running stitch with carpet thread along neckline. Insert body and draw up at neck. Tie securely in a bow.

Apron

Cut a piece of homespun 2½" x 4". Gather across top and knot off. Glue to body apron line on dress pattern.

Scarf

Cut ½" x 4" strip of homespun and gather along one long edge. Pull up gathers to form a fan shape. Tie off in a knot and glue on at neck. Glue cinnamon star on top of "fan".

Shawl
Cut a 1½" x 12" strip of homespun for shawl. Wrap around doll shoulders and glue at apron sides.

Hair & Face
Draw face with black and red pigment pens following features on body pattern. Color cheeks with blush and cotton swab. Sew curly grey hair on top of head. Glue miniature pencil to forehead.

Basket
Fill basket with Spanish moss, yarrow, apple, and other teacher goodies. Glue basket and items to top of apron.

Books
Paint wood books. Use colors that coordinate with dress fabric. Stack books together and secure with a drop of glue. Tie books together with a piece of jute. Knot tightly. Leave a 2" open space and knot again. Glue to apron where hands would appear to be.

Finishing Touches
Glue pencil to front of composition book. Glue book to front of doll. Glue pencil and ruler into wood pot and glue to front of doll above basket.

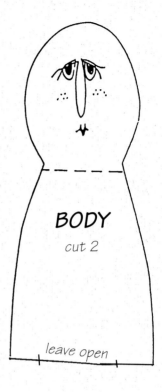

BODY

cut 2

leave open

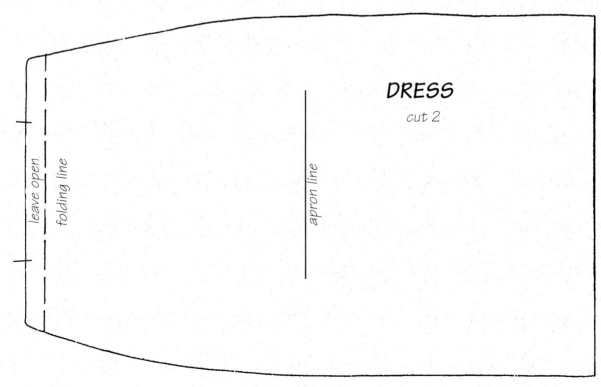

DRESS

cut 2

leave open

folding line

apron line

HOLLY DAYS

Mini Angels

Materials

Muslin: scrap (body)
Lace: flat, ⅜" (6")
Ribbon: paper twist, brown, 3"
Needle: hand-stitching
Stuffing
Thread: carpet; coordinating
Cinnamon star: small
Pigment pen: black, .01
Transfer tools
Toothpicks: pointed
Wire: covered, brown, 12"
Hot glue gun and glue sticks
Iron and ironing board
Scissors
Sewing machine
Cotton swabs
Powdered blush
Tube: ⅝" diameter

Read all instructions before beginning.

Body

Trace body pattern onto doubled piece of muslin. Stitch on line, leaving an opening where indicated. Cut ⅛" outside stitched line and turn right side out. Stuff firmly. Hand-stitch opening closed. Press arms to front. Place a drop of glue under each arm to hold in place. Glue cinnamon star to top of hands.

Face

Draw face with black pigment pen following features on body pattern. Color cheeks with blush and a cotton swab.

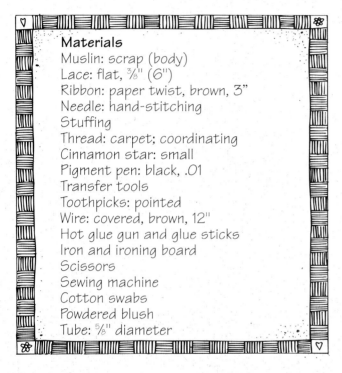

BODY

cut 2

leave open

Halo

Wrap center of brown covered wire around tube to form a base. Wrap each of the long ends of wire loosely around base, tightly wrapping tips around a pointed toothpick. Halo should resemble a grapevine wreath. Glue halo to angel's head.

Wings

Untwist paper ribbon until somewhat flat. Twist in center, and glue onto back of angel.

Finishing Touches

Glue flat lace around bottom of angel, starting and stopping in back. Loop carpet thread through top of head for ornament hanger.

QUILT ANGEL

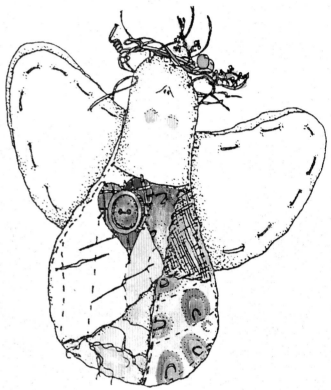

Materials

Muslin scrap: 3" x 8"
Quilt scrap: 4" x 8"
Paper ribbon: 4½" (optional/wings)
Batting
Button
Needle: hand-stitching
Stuffing
Thread: carpet; coordinating; linen
Doily: lace, round, 4" (optional/wings)
Pepperberries
Sweet Annie: sprig
Disappearing transfer pen
Pigment pen: black, .01
Transfer tools
Toothpicks
Covered wire: brown, 20"
Hot glue gun and glue sticks
Iron and ironing board
Scissors
Sewing machine
Cotton swabs
Powdered blush

Read all instructions before beginning.
Photo on pg. 94.

Body

With right sides together, sew 8" side of muslin to 8" side of quilt. Open out seam and press toward quilt. Fold piece in half with right sides together. Using disappearing transfer pen, trace body and head patterns (see pg. 99) on wrong side of muslin/quilt. Cut out heart pattern and hand-stitch onto body front. Sew body and head, leaving an opening where indicated. Cut ⅛" outside stitching line and turn right side out. Stuff firmly. Hand-stitch opening closed.

Face & Hair

Draw face with black pigment pen following Face Diagram (see pg. 99). Color cheeks with blush and cotton swab. Using linen thread, tie on pieces of hair around muslin part of head. Thread pieces through with a needle then tie off with a square knot, leaving ends about 1" long.

Halo

Wrap brown covered wire around lid of a 2 oz. paint bottle, having extra wire at each end to go back and wrap around. Wrap ends of wire loosely back around the circle to resemble a grapevine wreath. Wrap very end of each wire around end of a pointed toothpick to make a curly cue.

Wings (Cloth)

There are two options for wings. Using wings pattern, cut wings out of batting. Layer wings together. Using coordinating thread, make a primitive running stitch around outside edge. Glue to back of angel.

Wings (Doily)

Wings can be made from a gathered 4" doily (see instructions pg. 102) or paper ribbon. Cut a piece of matching paper ribbon 4½" long. Open out to its full width, then twist once in center. Glue to back of angel.

Finishing Touches

Glue halo neatly onto back of head. Add a few pepperberries and a sprig of sweet Annie. Glue a button on angel front. Using carpet thread, sew a loop on back of head to hang.

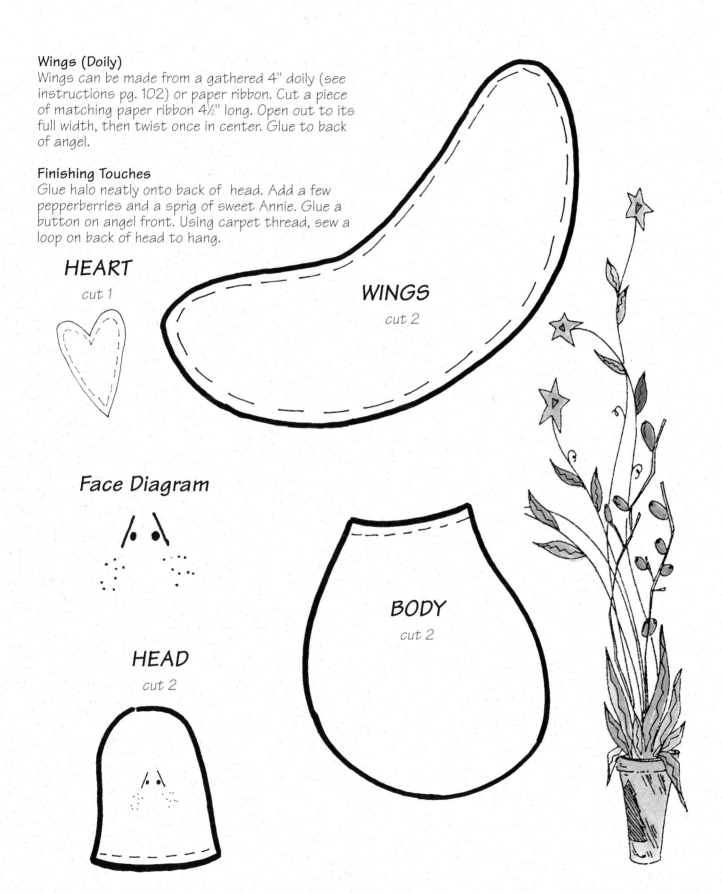

HEART
cut 1

WINGS
cut 2

Face Diagram

HEAD
cut 2

BODY
cut 2

Callie Christmas Angel

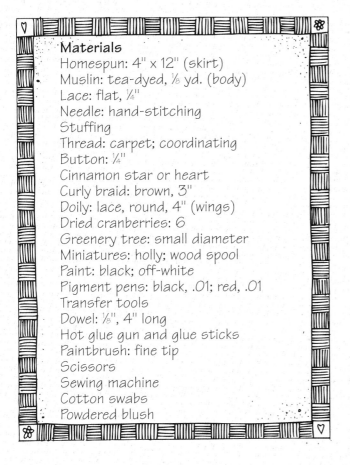

Materials
Homespun: 4" x 12" (skirt)
Muslin: tea-dyed, ⅛ yd. (body)
Lace: flat, ¼"
Needle: hand-stitching
Stuffing
Thread: carpet; coordinating
Button: ¼"
Cinnamon star or heart
Curly braid: brown, 3"
Doily: lace, round, 4" (wings)
Dried cranberries: 6
Greenery tree: small diameter
Miniatures: holly; wood spool
Paint: black; off-white
Pigment pens: black, .01; red, .01
Transfer tools
Dowel: ⅛", 4" long
Hot glue gun and glue sticks
Paintbrush: fine tip
Scissors
Sewing machine
Cotton swabs
Powdered blush

Read all instructions before beginning.

Body
Trace body pattern (see pg. 102) on doubled piece of muslin. Sew on line, leaving an opening where indicated. Cut ⅛" outside stitching, clipping curves and corners. Turn right side out. Stuff hands. Leave arms unstuffed. Firmly stuff body, head, and legs. Hand-stitch opening closed.

Paint
Paint upper body off-white. This becomes bodice of dress. Be accurate around neck and cuffs. With black paint, color on slippers (see Diagram 1).

Skirt
With right sides together, stitch homespun fabric 4" ends together. Turn right side out. Starting at center front, make a running stitch with a piece of carpet thread, leaving long ends to tie skirt on body. Glue flat lace at neckline and around arm cuffs, beginning and ending in back.

101

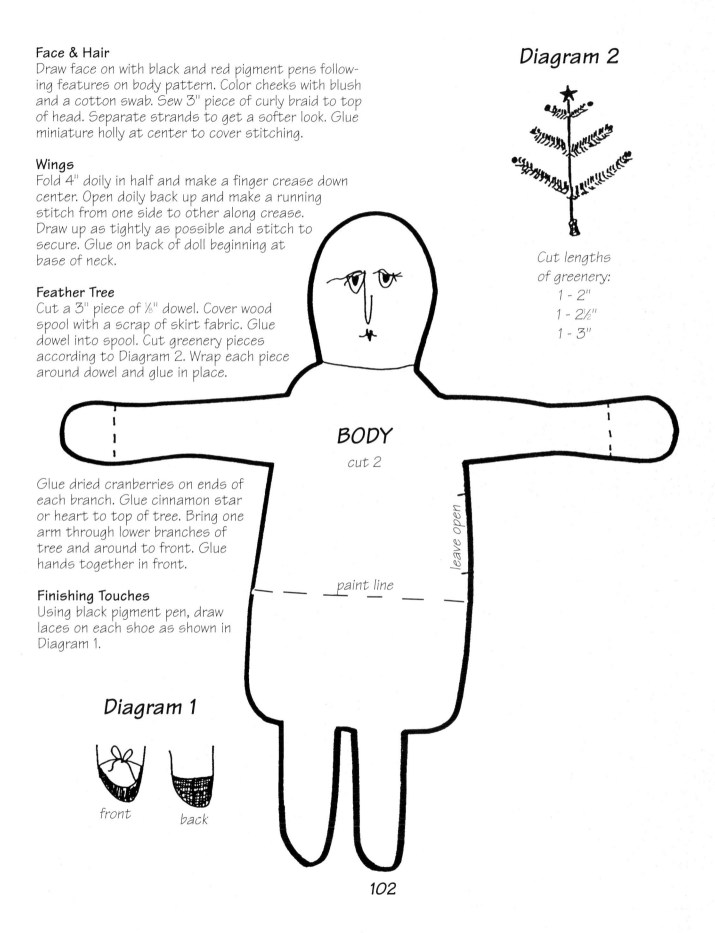

Face & Hair
Draw face on with black and red pigment pens following features on body pattern. Color cheeks with blush and a cotton swab. Sew 3" piece of curly braid to top of head. Separate strands to get a softer look. Glue miniature holly at center to cover stitching.

Wings
Fold 4" doily in half and make a finger crease down center. Open doily back up and make a running stitch from one side to other along crease. Draw up as tightly as possible and stitch to secure. Glue on back of doll beginning at base of neck.

Feather Tree
Cut a 3" piece of 1/8" dowel. Cover wood spool with a scrap of skirt fabric. Glue dowel into spool. Cut greenery pieces according to Diagram 2. Wrap each piece around dowel and glue in place.

Glue dried cranberries on ends of each branch. Glue cinnamon star or heart to top of tree. Bring one arm through lower branches of tree and around to front. Glue hands together in front.

Finishing Touches
Using black pigment pen, draw laces on each shoe as shown in Diagram 1.

Diagram 2

Cut lengths
of greenery:
1 - 2"
1 - 2½"
1 - 3"

BODY

cut 2

leave open

paint line

Diagram 1

front

back

102

Holly

Materials
Fabric: plaid, 1½" x 4" (apron)
Muslin: tea-dyed, 6" x 18" (body)
Lace: cotton, crocheted, ¼ yd.
Button: antique, small
Needle: hand-stitching
Stuffing
Thread: carpet; coordinating
Apple bits: dried
Artemesia
Canella berries: red
Cinnamon star
Doily: lace, round, 4"
Greens
Holly
Tansy
Wool roving: red (hair)
Paint: dk. green
Pigment pens: black, .01; red, .01
Transfer tools
Hot glue gun and glue sticks
Paintbrush: fine tip
Scissors
Sewing machine
Cotton swabs
Kitty litter: ½ cup
Powdered blush

Read all instructions before beginning.

Body
Trace body pattern (see pg. 105) on doubled piece of muslin. Sew on line, leaving opening where indicated. Cut ⅛" outside seam line. Make paper bag bottom (see General Instructions pg. 8). Turn right side out. Fill bottom with kitty litter; then stuff firmly. Referring to body pattern, paint body dk. green. Let dry.

Apron
Gather plaid fabric along one edge and draw up to 1½". Glue onto body (see apron line). Glue lace on at neckline, stopping and starting in back. Glue on a button at center of neck.

Face & Hair
Draw face with black and red pigment pens following features on body pattern. Color cheeks with blush and cotton swab. Sew red wool roving to top of head. Fluff out strands and glue a piece of holly over thread.

Wings
Fold 4" doily in half and make a finger crease down center. Open doily back up and make a running stitch from one side to other along crease. Draw up as tightly as possible and stitch to secure. Glue to back of doll beginning at base of neck.

Finishing Touches
Glue a variety of greens to one side of doll. Add a few sprigs of tansy and artemesia. Glue a cinnamon star at base of greens. String 1½" of dried apple pieces and attach to skirt. Glue a few red canella berries to cover top of apple strand.

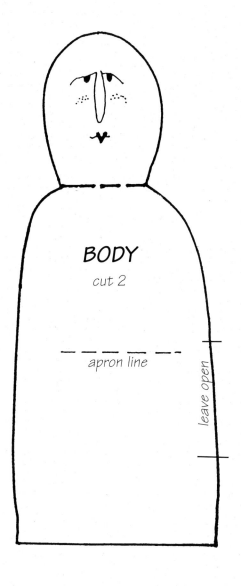

BODY

cut 2

- - - *apron line*

leave open

Be ye kind to one another, tenderhearted, forgiving one another, even as God for Christ's sake hath forgiven you.

Ephesians 4:32

Special Touches

ANGEL VEST

Materials
Vest pattern
Antique quilt: 6" x 8" (pocket)
Fabrics: lightweight
Homespun: contrasting (lining)
Muslin: pre-quilted (vest)
Muslin: 3½" x 3" (flower patch)
Muslin: (large angel)
Lace: flat, 3"; 4½"
Floss: blue; gold; red; coordinating
Needles: hand-stitching; embroidery
Thread: coordinating
Buttons: 8
Loopy yarn or wavy wool (hair)
Doilies: crocheted, round, 4"; lace, round, 3"
Fusible web
Disappearing transfer pen
Pigment pens: black, .01; red, .01
Transfer tools
Iron and ironing board
Scissors
Sewing machine
Cotton swabs
Powdered blush

Read all instructions before beginning.

Use a simple commercial vest pattern. Use pre-quilted muslin for outside and homespun for lining. Muslin can be tea-dyed. Any vest or shirt will adapt.

Pocket
Cut a piece of muslin 6" x 8". With right sides together, stitch muslin and antique quilt together, leaving a 1" opening to turn. Clip corners and turn right side out. Press. Place pocket on left, front side of vest. Sew onto vest.

Flower Patch
Pre-wash a 3½" X 3" piece of muslin. Sew on a row of flowers in various heights and sizes with floss (see Flower Patch Diagram on pg. 113). Stitch on buttons for flower heads. Press under each edge ¼". Hand-stitch, using primitive running stitch, to chosen spot on vest. Use a dark floss to sew patch onto vest for a more dramatic effect.

Quilt Star
Using Quilt Star pattern (see pg. 110), cut 3 or 4 stars out of different fabrics or quilt remnants and hand-stitch onto vest. Outline star pattern randomly on front and back of vest with a disappearing transfer pen; stitch outline with gold and red floss.

Small Angel

Body
Cut out, body 1, leg 1, and head 1 patterns. Trace pieces onto fusible webbing. Fuse body on wrong side of quilt and head and legs on muslin. Cut out on traced line.

Wings
Cut 4" crocheted or soft doily in half, and gather along cut edges for wings. Peel off paper on body piece and position on right, front bottom of vest. Before pressing piece, stick edges of wings, head, and legs under body piece. Press with iron according to manufacturer's instructions.

Stitching
Applique around head and legs with satin stitch and matching thread. Machine-stitch quilt piece with a small straight stitch close to edge. Hand-tack wings so they do not flop down. Cut a 3" piece of flat lace and hand-stitch to bottom of body. Cut another small piece of lace and gather. Tack at neck and sew on button at center.

Slippers
Draw on slippers and bows with a black pigment pen (see foot 1).

Face & Hair
Draw face with black and red pigment pens (see head 1). Color cheeks with blush and a cotton swab. Sew 2" piece of looped yarn or wavy wool on for hair. Sew a button over center to cover stitching.

Finishing Touches
Sew three buttons down front of body.

FOOT 1

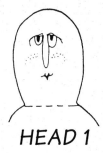

LEG 1

cut 2

HEAD 1

QUILT STAR

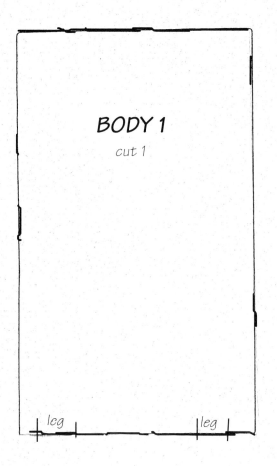

BODY 1

cut 1

leg   leg

Large Angel

Body
Trace wings pattern (see pg. 77), body 2, leg 2, and head 2 onto fusible webbing. Fuse body on wrong side of quilt and head and legs on muslin. Satin stitch head and legs in matching colors.

Wings
Fuse wings to a light fabric. Make a primitive running stitch around wings. Sew onto quilt body with a straight stitch close to edge.

Dressing
Cut a piece of lace 4½" long and stitch along bottom of body. Sew three large buttons up the front. Cut 3" doily in half and stitch on at neck. Stitch button at center neckline.

Face & Hair
Draw face with black and red pigment pens (see head 2). Color cheeks with blush and a cotton swab. Stitch a 3" piece of hair on top of head . Sew a button over center to cover stitching.

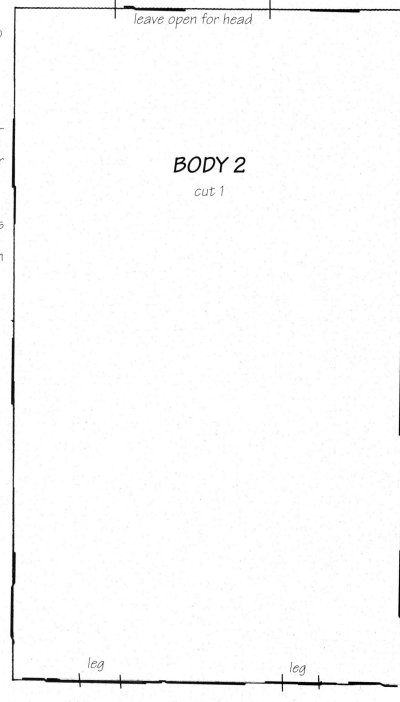

LEG 2

cut 2

leave open for head

BODY 2

cut 1

leg   leg

HEAD 2

QUILT BAG...

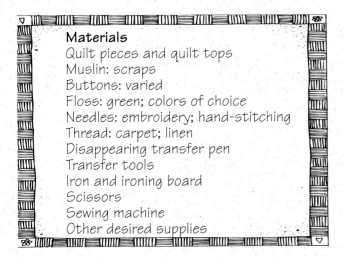

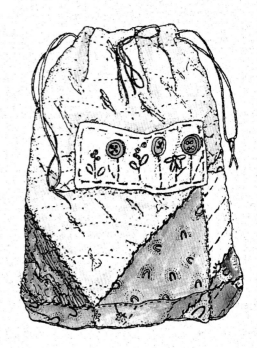

Materials
Quilt pieces and quilt tops
Muslin: scraps
Buttons: varied
Floss: green; colors of choice
Needles: embroidery; hand-stitching
Thread: carpet; linen
Disappearing transfer pen
Transfer tools
Iron and ironing board
Scissors
Sewing machine
Other desired supplies

Read all instructions before beginning.

Quilt bags can be made out of old homespun quilt tops, and quilts. Size and shapes can vary to fit with available pieces and sizes. An average bag ranges between 5" x 5" and 5" x 7".

Bag
Cut quilt piece to desired width and two times desired length. Fold piece with right sides together and stitch side seams. Turn right side out and press. Turn top raw edge under ½" and make a running stitch with linen thread. Leave long ends to draw up and tie off in a bow.

Patches
To cover worn areas or add design, make patches on muslin, then stitch onto bags. Use Flower Patch Diagram for reference. Make patches wider or narrower to suit project.

Flower Patch
Using the Flower Patch Diagram, trace design onto muslin with disappearing transfer pen. Using green floss make a primitive running stitch for flower stems and lazy daisies for leaves. Other flowers can be added with various floss colors and French knots or lazy daisy stitches. Sew on buttons for flower heads. When patch is finished, cut down evenly to fit onto bag. Turn under edges and press. With carpet thread or floss, make a running stitch around outside edge to secure patch onto bag.

Flower Patch Diagram

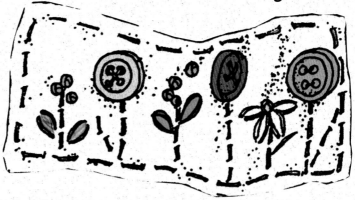

113

GRACE APPLIQUE...

Materials
Sweatshirt or vest
Fabric scraps: brown (arms);
       orange (nose); seed
       packet design
Flannel: ¼ yd. (body)
Old quilt: scrap (shawl)
Homespun: scrap (hair bow)
Raffia
Buttons: old, ½" (4); ⅜" (1)
Floss: various
Needle: hand-stitching
Thread: coordinating
Charm: small birdhouse
Fusible applique
Pigment pen: black, .01
Transfer tools
Iron and ironing board
Scissors
Sewing machine
Cotton swabs
Powdered blush
Safety pin

Read all instructions before beginning.

Grace can be appliqued to a number of different items. The pattern pieces on pg. 116 are for a child's sweatshirt. Patterns can be enlarged for an adult sweatshirt or shrunk to fit a tea towel or tote bag.

Body
Enlarge and cut all pattern pieces (see pg. 116). Cut 2" X 20" flannel scrap or quilt piece for scarf. Fold around neck to look like scarf. Following instructions for fusible applique (see pg. 9), place body piece with scarf on project. Machine-stitch around body with a satin stitch. Straight stitch scarf close to edge to secure it. Satin stitch around arms and nose.

Face & Hair
Draw face with black and red pigment pens following features on body pattern. The eyes can also be done with floss and French knots (see General Instructions pg. 8). Color cheeks with blush and cotton swab. Use a designer stitch on sewing machine to sew on hair.

Basket
Use a textured brown print for basket. Many new fabrics have seed packets printed on them; they work well to cut out and stitch into the basket. Satin stitch seed packets into basket. Tie basket to arm by making a raffia bow and pinning it underneath so it appears basket has been tied to stick arm. Run a thread through birdhouse charm and tie to front of basket.

Finishing Touches
Cut strip of homespun and tie into a bow. Tack bow between branches of hair. Sew a button into center. Sew 4 buttons down body front. Sew a larger button on overlap of scarf. Dry clean or hand-wash project.

Enlarge all pattern pieces to 125% for child's sweatshirt.

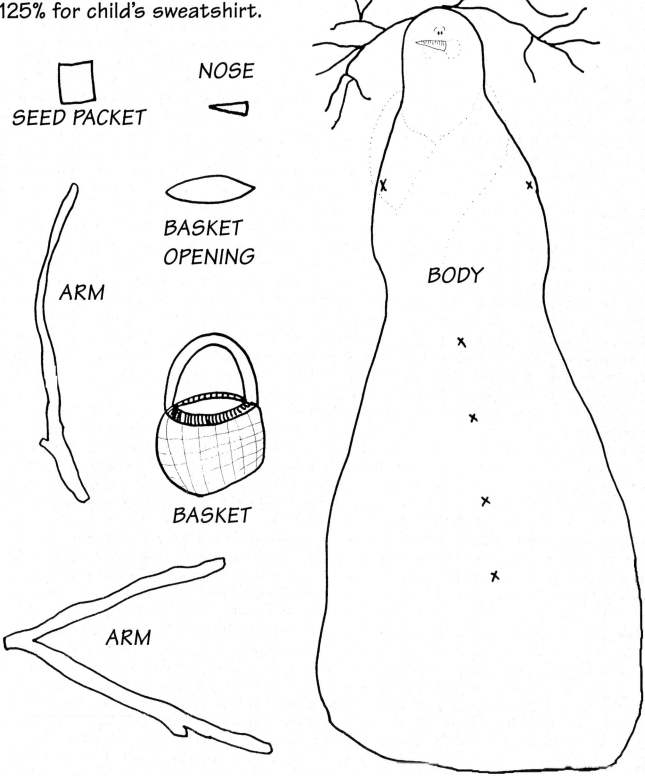

SEED PACKET

NOSE

BASKET OPENING

ARM

BASKET

ARM

BODY

Friends Quilt

Materials
Fabric: 18" x 26" (backing)
Fabric: 9-12 various scraps
Osnaburg: 6" x 5"
Raffia
Batting: 16" x 24"
Buttons: assorted
Floss: 3-4 colors
Needles: embroidery; hand-stitching
Straight pins
Stuffing (pillow)
Thread: coordinating
Assorted embellishments
Transfer tools
Wood branch: 20"
Iron and ironing board
Scissors
Sewing machine

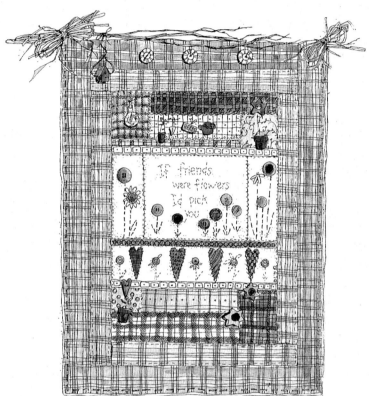

Read all instructions before beginning.
(approximate size of quilt 16" x 25")

Center
Transfer Center Piece Diagram (see pg. 120) onto osnaburg and Heart Diagram onto scraps (see pg. 121). Embroider stems. Cut eight 1" squares of various fabrics. Fold corners into center to form flower. Sew button in center of each flower and secure to quilt at top of each stem. Wipe off extra transfer marks. Press stitched piece.

Piecing
Cut quilt pieces out of various scraps (see patterns pg. 119). Using center piece as an anchor, hand-stitch quilt pieces together (see Piecing Diagram pg. 121). If machine-stitching add ¼" seam allowance to pattern pieces. Pin together before sewing. Stitch a 1½" border of scrap fabric around entire piece. Once sewn together, hand-stitch

desired stitches with floss around each border. Refer to General Instructions (pg. 8) and Stitching Guide (pg. 119) for stitches that can be used.

Accessories
Fill in squares with assorted embellishments: flower pot buttons, heart-shaped wood buttons, tiny baskets, and tin charms. Cut out heart shapes from various fabrics. Add patch hearts and primitively stitch them on (see Heart Diagram pg. 121). Leave a 2" border of base fabric around all sides.

Quilt
Cut batting to size of top and a backing fabric the same size. Sandwich batting in between front and back. Make a running stitch through all layers.

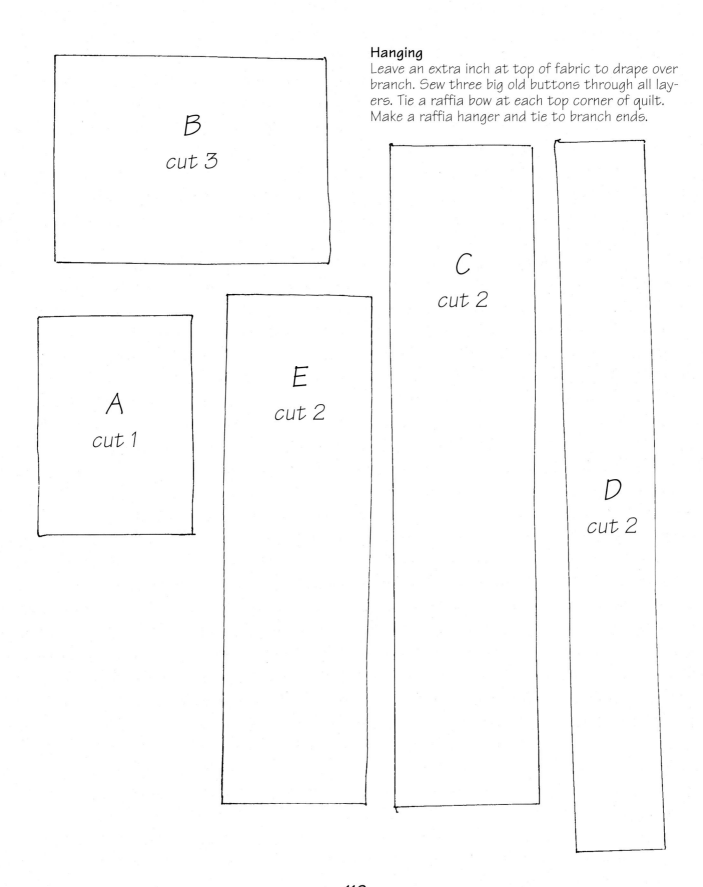

Hanging
Leave an extra inch at top of fabric to drape over branch. Sew three big old buttons through all layers. Tie a raffia bow at each top corner of quilt. Make a raffia hanger and tie to branch ends.

B

cut 3

A

cut 1

E

cut 2

C

cut 2

D

cut 2

Center Piece Diagram

enlarge to 110%

If friends were flowers I'd pick you

Flowers

Primitive Running Stitch

Piecing Diagram

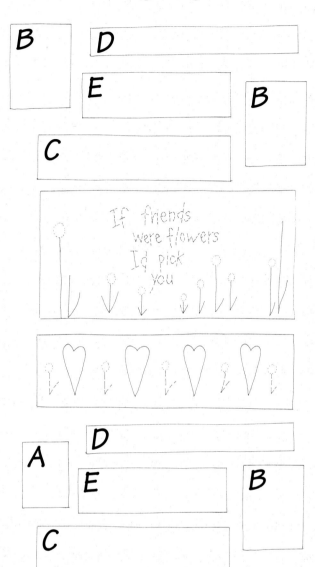

B

D

E

B

C

If friends
were flowers
I'd pick
you

D

A

E

B

C

Stitching Guide

Cross-stitch

(D) (B)

(A) (C)

Herringbone Stitch

(C) (B) (G) (F)

(A) (E) (D) (H)

Blanket Stitch

(1)

(B)

(A) (C)

(2)

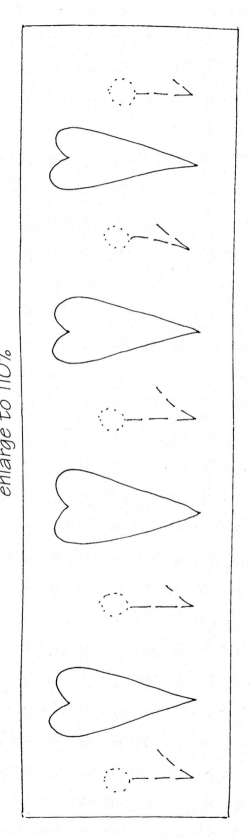

Heart Diagram

enlarge to 110%

121

Walter

Materials

Homespun: plaid, ⅛ yd. (vest)
Homespun: ½ yd. (hat)
Homespun: scrap (fish)
Muslin: ½ yd.
Button
Floss: black; coordinating
Jute
Needles: embroidery; hand-stitching
Straight pins
Stuffing
Thread: carpet; coordinating
Spanish moss
Paint: burnt orange
Disappearing transfer pen
Pigment pen: black, .01
Transfer tools
Sticks
Oven-bake clay: white
Fishing basket: small
Hot glue gun and glue sticks
Iron and ironing board
Paintbrush: fine tip
Paring knife
Scissors
Sewing machine
Cotton swabs
Kitty litter: 1 cup
Powdered blush

Read all instruction before beginning.

Body
Enlarge and trace around body pattern (see pg. 126) on doubled piece of muslin. Sew on line leaving an opening where indicated. Cut ⅛" outside seam and turn right side out. Fill bottom with kitty litter. Stuff firmly. Hand-stitch opening closed.

Vest
Cut vest fronts and back (see pgs. 124-125) out of plaid homespun. Sew side seams, leaving a small opening for the stick arms to poke through. Press side seams open. Turn raw edges under ¼" and stitch with a primitive running stitch using coordinating floss. Place on body and secure with glue.

Hunting Cap
Cut out hat bill, hat band and ear flaps (see pg. 124-125). Sew hat bills and ear flaps on traced lines. Leave openings where indicated. Cut out and turn right sides out. Press. Pin hat bill where indicated on right side of hat band. Pin flaps

where shown in each side of bill. Hand baste all pieces in place. Pin one hat band to other band, right sides together, and stitch on seam line. Pull out hand basting. Press band seam one way. Sew seam. Press out bill and flaps. Using carpet thread, gather top edge ¼" from unfinished edge. Draw up tightly and tie off. Turn right side out. Glue a button to top of hat.

Face

Using body pattern (see pg. 126) make French knots for eyes and a primitive running stitch for mouth with black floss. (See General Instructions pg. 8.) Color cheeks with blush and a cotton swab.

Nose

Roll a piece of oven-bake clay into a "snake" shape to a diameter of about ¼". Cut a 1" piece. Roll one end to a blunt point and flatten the other end. Make random lines with a paring knife along sides of the nose. Bake according to manufacturer's instructions. Let cool. Paint burnt orange. Let dry. Glue to face just below eyes.

Fish

Trace fish pattern on doubled piece of homespun. Stitch on line, leaving opening at tail. Cut out and turn right side out. Stuff firmly. Hand-stitch opening closed.

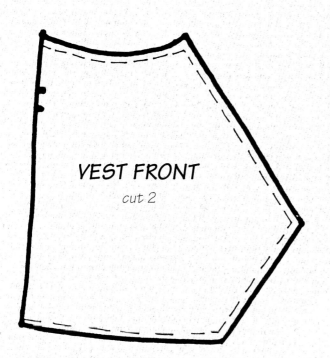

VEST FRONT

cut 2

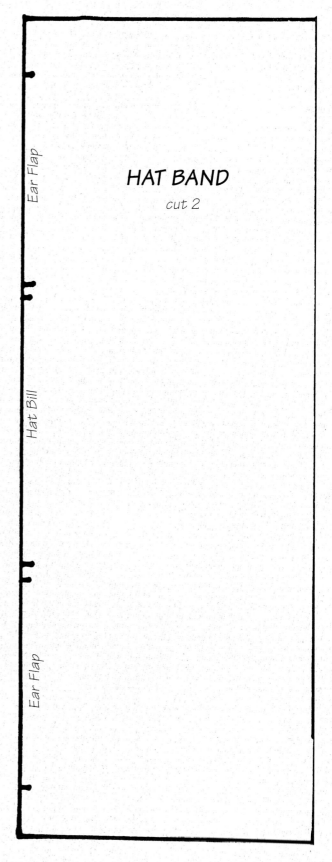

Ear Flap

Hat Bill

Ear Flap

HAT BAND

cut 2

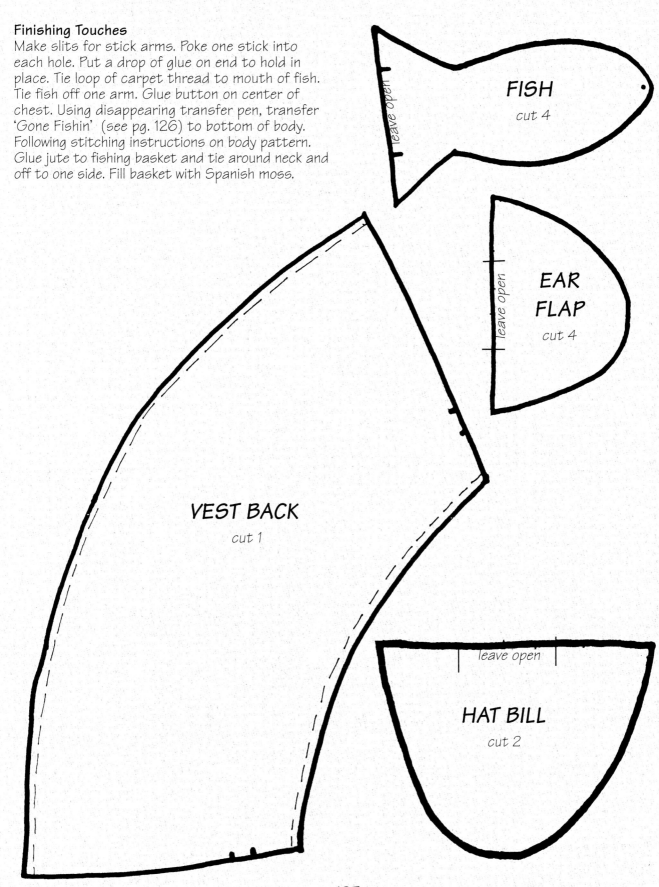

Finishing Touches

Make slits for stick arms. Poke one stick into each hole. Put a drop of glue on end to hold in place. Tie loop of carpet thread to mouth of fish. Tie fish off one arm. Glue button on center of chest. Using disappearing transfer pen, transfer 'Gone Fishin' (see pg. 126) to bottom of body. Following stitching instructions on body pattern. Glue jute to fishing basket and tie around neck and off to one side. Fill basket with Spanish moss.

FISH
cut 4

leave open

EAR
FLAP
cut 4

leave open

VEST BACK
cut 1

leave open

HAT BILL
cut 2

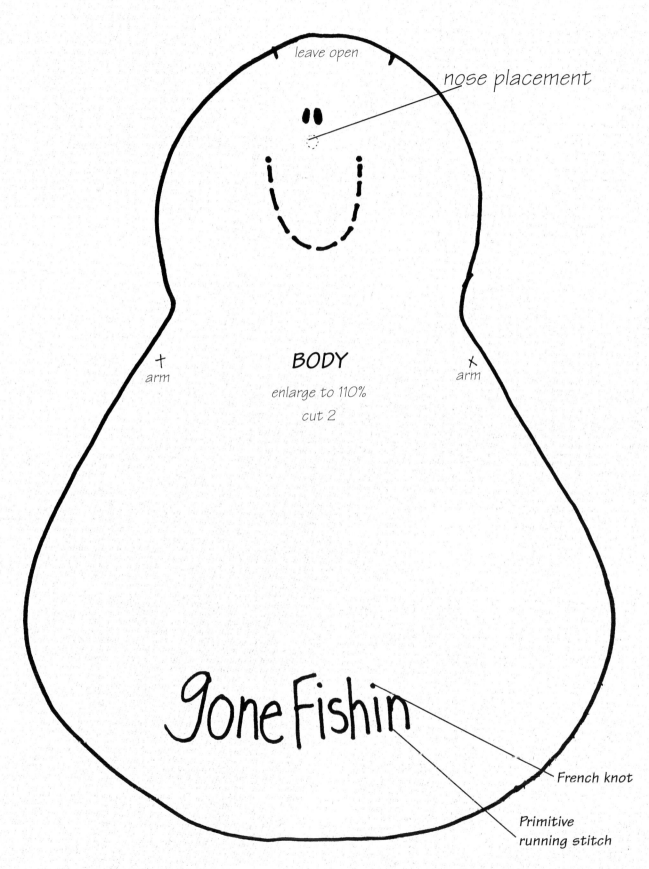

leave open

nose placement

BODY

enlarge to 110%

cut 2

† arm

† arm

gone Fishin

French knot

Primitive
running stitch

EQUIVALENCY CHART

INCHES TO MILLIMETRES AND CENTIMETRES

INCHES	MM	CM	INCHES	CM	INCHES	CM
⅛	3	0.9	9	22.9	30	76.2
¼	6	0.6	10	25.4	31	78.7
⅜	10	1.0	11	27.9	32	81.3
½	13	1.3	12	30.5	33	83.8
⅝	16	1.6	13	33.0	34	86.4
¾	19	1.9	14	35.6	35	88.9
⅞	22	2.2	15	38.1	36	91.4
1	25	2.5	16	40.6	37	94.0
1¼	32	3.2	17	43.2	38	96.5
1½	38	3.8	18	45.7	39	99.1
1¾	44	4.4	19	48.3	40	101.6
2	51	5.1	20	50.8	41	104.1
2½	64	6.4	21	53.3	42	106.7
3	76	7.6	22	55.9	43	109.2
3½	89	8.9	23	58.4	44	111.8
4	102	10.2	24	61.0	45	114.3
4½	114	11.4	25	63.5	46	116.8
5	127	12.7	26	66.0	47	119.4
6	152	15.2	27	68.6	48	121.9
7	178	17.8	28	71.1	49	124.5
8	203	20.3	29	73.7	50	127.0

YARDS TO METRES

YARDS	METRES	YARDS	METRES	YARDS	METRES	YARDS	METRES	YARDS	METRES
⅛	0.11	2⅛	1.94	41/8	3.77	6⅛	5.60	8⅛	7.43
¼	0.23	2¼	2.06	41/4	3.89	6¼	5.72	8¼	7.54
⅜	0.34	2⅜	2.17	43/8	4.00	6⅜	5.83	8⅜	7.66
½	0.46	2½	2.29	41/2	4.11	6½	5.94	8½	7.77
⅝	0.57	2⅝	2.40	45/8	4.23	6⅝	6.06	8⅝	7.89
¾	0.69	2¾	2.51	43/4	4.34	6¾	6.17	8¾	8.00
⅞	0.80	2⅞	2.63	47/8	4.46	6⅞	6.29	8⅞	8.12
1	0.91	3	2.74	5	4.57	7	6.40	9	8.23
1⅛	1.03	3⅛	2.86	51/8	4.69	7⅛	6.52	9⅛	8.34
1¼	1.14	3¼	2.97	51/4	4.80	7¼	6.63	9¼	8.46
1⅜	1.26	3⅜	3.09	53/8	4.91	7⅜	6.74	9⅜	8.57
1½	1.37	3½	3.20	51/2	5.03	7½	6.86	9½	8.69
1⅝	1.49	3⅝	3.31	55/8	5.14	7⅝	6.97	9⅝	8.80
1¾	1.60	3¾	3.43	53/4	5.26	7¾	7.09	9¾	8.92
1⅞	1.71	3⅞	3.54	57/8	5.37	7⅞	7.20	9⅞	9.03
2	1.83	4	3.66	6	5.49	8	7.32	10	9.14

INDEX